You

The Vietnam War
A History in Documents

The Vietnam War
A History in Documents

Marilyn B. Young
John J. Fitzgerald
A. Tom Grunfeld

OXFORD
UNIVERSITY PRESS

To our students

OXFORD
UNIVERSITY PRESS

Oxford New York

Auckland Bangkok Buenos Aires Cape Town
Chennai Dar es Salaam Delhi Hong Kong Istambul Karachi
Kolkata Kuala Lumpur Madrid Melbourne Mexico City Mumbai
Nairobi São Paulo Shanghai Singapore Taipei Tokyo Toronto
with an associated company in Berlin

Copyright © 2002 by Marilyn B. Young,
John J. Fitzgerald, and A. Tom Grunfeld

Design: Sandy Kaufman
Layout: Loraine Machlin
Picture Research: Jennifer Smith

Published by Oxford University Press, Inc.
198 Madison Avenue, New York, New York 10016
www.oup.com

Library of Congress Cataloging in Publication Data
Young, Marilyn Blatt
The Vietnam War: a history in documents /
Marilyn B. Young, John J. Fitzgerald, A. Tom Grunfeld
p. cm. — (Pages from history)
Includes bibliographical references and index.
ISBN: 0-19-512278-X
1. Vietnamese Conflict, 1961–1975-History-Sources. I. Fitzgerald, John J.
II. Grunfeld, A. Tom III. Title. IV. Series.
DS557.7 .Y677 2002
959.704'3-dc21
2001052338

Printed in the United States of America on acid-free paper

General Editors

Sarah Deutsch
Associate Professor of History
University of Arizona

Carol K. Karlsen
Professor of History
University of Michigan

Robert G. Moeller
Professor of History
University of California, Irvine

Jeffrey N. Wasserstrom
Associate Professor of History
Indiana University

Board of Advisors

Steven Goldberg
Social Studies Supervisor
New Rochelle, N.Y., Public Schools

John Pyne
Social Studies Supervisor
West Milford, N.J., Public Schools

Cover photo: *Suspected Viet Cong base camp being destroyed by the U.S. Army.*

Cover border text: *Excerpt from a South Vietnamese song*

Frontispiece: *U.S. soldiers, Long Khanh province, Republic of Vietnam, 1966*

Title page: *A Chinese poster rallying support for the North Vietnamese forces.*

Contents page: *John J. Fitzgerald's "dog tags"*

Contents

What Is a Document?

To the historian, a document is, quite simply, any sort of historical evidence. It is a primary source, the raw material of history. A document may be more than the expected government paperwork, such as a treaty or passport. It is also a letter, diary, will, grocery list, newspaper article, recipe, memoir, oral history, school yearbook, map, chart, architectural plan, poster, musical score, play script, novel, political cartoon, painting, photograph—even an object.

Using primary sources allows us not just to read *about* history, but to read history itself. It allows us to immerse ourselves in the look and feel of an era gone by, to understand its people and their language, whether verbal or visual. And it allows us to take an active, hands-on role in (re)constructing history.

Using primary sources requires us to use our powers of detection to ferret out the relevant facts and to draw conclusions from them; just as Agatha Christie uses the scores in a bridge game to determine the identity of a murderer, the historian uses facts from a variety of sources—some, perhaps, seemingly inconsequential—to build a historical case.

The poet W. H. Auden wrote that history was the study of questions. Primary sources force us to ask questions—and then, by answering them, to construct a narrative or an argument that makes sense to us. Moreover, as we draw on the many sources from "the dust-bin of history," we can endow that narrative with character, personality, and texture—all the elements that make history so endlessly intriguing.

Cartoon
This political cartoon addresses the issue of church and state. It illustrates the Supreme Court's role in balancing the demands of the First Amendment of the Constitution and the desires of the religious population.

Illustration
Illustrations from children's books, such as this alphabet from the New England Primer, tell us how children were educated, and also what the religious and moral values of the time were.

A — In *Adam's* Fall We Sinned all.

B — Thy Life to Mend This *Book* Attend.

C — The *Cat* doth play And after slay.

D — A *Dog* will bite A Thief at night.

E — An *Eagles* flight Is out of sight.

Treaty

A government document such as this 1805 treaty can reveal not only the details of government policy, but information about the people who signed it. Here, the Indians' names were written in English transliteration by U.S. officials; the Indians added pictographs to the right of their names.

Map

A 1788 British map of India shows the region prior to British colonization, an indication of the kingdoms and provinces whose ethnic divisions would resurface later in India's history.

Literature

The first written version of the Old English epic *Beowulf*, from the late 10th century, is physical evidence of the transition from oral to written history. Charred by fire, it is also a physical record of the wear and tear of history.

How to Read a Document

The documents in this book reflect many different aspects of the history of the Vietnam War. Some of the documents are drawn from Vietnam's long record of nationalist resistance to foreign domination, its position in the 19th century as a French colony, and its 30-year war of independence against first the French and then the Americans. Others are devoted to the involvement of the United States in Vietnam. The sources include government documents, poems, letters, memoirs, war journalism, photography, and cartoons. The documents reflect the extent to which U.S. involvement in Vietnam, which began quietly and without much public attention in the 1950s, came to absorb all of American society over the following decades.

The Vietnam War, as Americans call it (the Vietnamese call it the American War), was among the most divisive episodes in American history. Policy makers in the U.S. Presidential administrations who slowly escalated the war believed they were acting in the best interests of the United States. And those who opposed them, an ever-larger number of people—not just in the United States, but throughout the world—were equally certain the war served no honorable purpose. Even today, so long after peace has been established, memories of the war continue to haunt many Americans and Vietnamese. To read these documents accurately, it is important to try to imagine the passion with which many of them were written and the anger they evoked.

Expression

Photographs can be understood in many different ways. Their power is that they seem to tell us about something that really happened. Yet they do not interpret themselves. The viewer must "read" the image. The photograph on the opposite page was a common one to American newspaper readers and television viewers throughout the years of the war. The young marine looks serious and determined. He is well armed and equipped. He guards a group of poorly dressed women, children, and old men whose faces express fear and concern. They are watchful, waiting, and powerless.

Point of View

Because the soldier is guarding the group, the viewer must assume they are dangerous. Yet the image is also disturbing. The Vietnamese seem to be ordinary villagers. Are these the enemy? Where are their guns? If these helpless looking villagers are the enemy, why is it taking so long to defeat them? A photograph like this was read differently by those who supported and those who opposed the war. If you identify yourself with the marine, you are sympathetic to the problem of fighting a war in which you cannot be sure who is your friend, who your foe. If you identify with the villagers, the marine is a figure of fear and oppression.

Irony

Tom Lehrer was a popular songwriter and performer in the 1950s and 1960s whose commentary on current events delighted those who agreed with him. Lehrer incorporates both popular cultural images and official explanations for U.S. intervention in his mocking praise of intervention. The government argued that U.S. troops were in Vietnam to protect people's rights; Lehrer's song makes fun of this simply by repeating it. Unlike the photograph, the song is unambiguous.

Caricature

This 1983 cartoon comments on the legacies of the war. One reason given for the long delay in normalizing relations between the United States and Vietnam was the charge that Vietnam continued to imprison American prisoners of war. The artist has a different notion of who is actually a prisoner of war: wounded veterans, veterans suffering nightmare memories of their combat experience, and the American military itself. The veterans are drawn with great sympathy. The military officers, on the other hand, are broadly caricatured as they look at the possible locations for future wars. Cartoons, unlike photographs, are rarely ambiguous. They represent the views of the artist in the same way an editorial or an essay does.

CONTINUING PRISONERS OF THE VIETNAM WAR.

Greenberg — Daily News, Los Angeles '83

Send the Marines

When someone makes a move
Of which we don't approve,
Who is it that always intervenes?
U.N. and O.A.S.,
They have their place, I guess,
But first send the Marines!

We'll send them all we've got,
John Wayne and Randolph Scott,
Remember those exciting fighting scenes?
From the halls of Montezuma
To show our sense of huma
What do we do? Send in the Marines!

For might makes right,
And till they've seen the light,
They've got to be protected,
All their rights respected,
Till somebody we like can be elected.

Members of the corps
All hate the thought of war,
They'd rather kill them off by peaceful means.
Stop calling it aggression,
We hate that expression.
We only want the world to know
That we support the status quo,
They love us ev'rywhere we go,
So when in doubt, send the Marines!

MAP OF
INDO-CHINA.

SCALE OF STATUTE MILES.

0   50 100   200   300   400

A Little History, by Way of Introduction

The country we know today as Vietnam had its origins some 2,000 years ago when the Viet people began moving southward from China into what is now northern Vietnam, absorbing or pushing further south the aboriginal Malay people they encountered there. In 111 B.C., not long after the Viets had settled in their new home, Chinese armies arrived to colonize them, calling their land Nam Viet (Land of the Southern Viets).

The 1,000-year Chinese rule left an indelible cultural imprint on the Vietnamese, who adopted and incorporated into their own society many aspects of the country that had ruled them. These included the written script, the form of central government administration, and an approach to governing, family life, and social relations named after the 6th century B.C. philosopher, Confucius. Vietnam's adoption of elements of Chinese culture, coupled with its resentment of Chinese colonization, defined a Vietnamese ambivalence toward China that remains to this day. Buddhism also came to Vietnam by way of China, introduced into the country by Chinese monks fleeing disorders at home in the 2nd century A.D. and by pilgrims traveling between China and India. Especially popular among the peasantry, Buddhism became the major religion of Vietnam.

Although impressed by China as a political model, the Vietnamese ruling elite never fully accepted Chinese political control and mounted repeated rebellions to attain their independence. In the 10th century they were successful and, with considerable pride, named their

A depiction of Confucius, 6th century B.C. Chinese philosopher. The text of this painting speaks of a virtuous society structured on the Confucian ideals of selflessness, respect, and duty.

Confucian culture

Confucianism, as Western scholars call it, sees government and society as extensions of the family and its values. It was the task of the emperor and his officials to preserve these values through ritual obligations that ordered society along hierarchical lines. Thus, younger brothers must defer to older brothers, children to fathers, women to men, and, by the same logic, subjects to officials and officials to the emperor. The system rested on the moral behavior of superiors to those below them and the loyalty of the subordinates to those above them. Officials were to be chosen for government service by merit, demonstrated by success in an elaborate system of examinations based on Confucian philosophy. The emperor, however, usually came to power by force and established his family as hereditary rulers (called a dynasty) until, in turn, he was overthrown.

country Dai Viet (Greater State of Viet). But independence did not guarantee freedom from invasion, and the Vietnamese were forced to fight off repeated Chinese and Mongol invasions over the next 700 years.

Starting in the 11th century, the people of Dai Viet slowly expanded their territory in what the Vietnamese call the March South (Nam Tien). In a series of bloody battles in the late 15th century, led by the Le Dynasty, the Vietnamese conquered all of the Kingdom of Champa and annexed its territory.

Rivalry between two powerful families in the 17th century led to civil war and division of the country between the two: the Trinh in the north and the Nguyen in the south. But both the Trinh and the Nguyen continued to swear fealty to the Le Dynasty, whose rule was largely ceremonial. The March South continued and Vietnamese settlers moved deep into the Mekong Delta, then part of the Khmer kingdom. By the late 18th century Vietnam, although still politically divided between the Nguyen and the Trinh, had assumed the S-shaped contours with which we are now familiar.

European explorers, merchants, and missionaries had begun appearing on Vietnam's shores in the 16th century. Although trade was slow to develop, by the 17th century vigorous French missionaries, with their message of a Kingdom of God that was superior to any earthly empire, threatened Confucian beliefs and aroused hostility and repression in both parts of the country.

Towards the end of the 18th century, there was growing discontent with the Trinh rule in the south and the Nguyen in the north. Government corruption, unequal land distribution, heavy taxation, unrest among ethnic minorities in the mountains, and a series of natural disasters combined to create a full-scale peasant rebellion. It was led by the Tay Son brothers (named after their southern village), who promised social and economic reforms and the restoration of the Le Dynasty to actual, rather than nominal, rule. The Tay Son defeated both the Trinh and the Nguyen forces, and united the country. The most powerful of the brothers established a dynasty in his own name, but with his death, an heir of the defeated Nguyen family resumed the war.

In 1802, Nguyen Anh, aided by a French missionary surprisingly skilled in military matters, defeated the Tay Son and declared himself emperor. Taking the imperial name Gia Long, Nguyen Anh made the city of Hue, in Central Vietnam, the new capital of the country, modeling its architecture on Beijing, imperial capital of China.

Despite the help Nguyen Anh had received from his French missionary supporters, he was wary of French activities; his son and successor, Minh Mang, went further, attempting to throw missionaries out of the country altogether and instituting a harsh persecution of Vietnamese converts. The French response was not long in coming. Spurred by its colonial rivalry with Great Britain and angered by Vietnamese policies towards missionaries, France opened military hostilities against the Vietnamese in the 1850s. In 1862, the Emperor Tu Duc ceded three southern provinces to the French, who promptly named the region Cochin China (the name came from the word early Portuguese explorers had given to Vietnam), ruling it as a colony until 1945.

By 1884 the French had gained control of all of Vietnam along with neighboring Cambodia and Laos, referring to the entire area as French Indochina. Vietnam itself was further divided into two protectorates that the French named Tonkin for the north (the word originates from the French phonetic pronunciation of a Sino-Vietnamese word meaning "eastern capital") and Annam (the old Chinese designation for the "pacified South") for central Vietnam.

The French believed they were on a *mission civilisatrice* (civilizing mission), despite the conviction of many Vietnamese that they were already civilized and indeed in possession of a civilization superior to anything the French had to offer. What Vietnam lacked, however, was the means to protect itself against a superior military and industrial power. From the first, there were organized rebellions against the French led by the displaced Vietnamese ruling elite, each bringing in the wake of its failure ever more stringent repression. Meanwhile, the French transformed Vietnamese society from the inside out, introducing new forms of taxation, new patterns of landowning, new industries that exploited the land, and new social classes. At the top of these new social classes were French civil servants, at the bottom, Vietnamese peasants, many now landless farmers.

Some economic development occurred under French rule, but its goal was limited to increasing trade between France and Vietnam. Local industries that might compete with France were discouraged in favor of a more efficient extraction of raw materials. Under the French, rice production increased, but this meant greater exports, not more rice for Vietnamese consumption.

A Note on Spelling

Vietnamese is a tonal language in which homonyms—words that are pronounced alike—are distinguished by rising, falling, and flat tones. The written form of the language used Chinese characters until the 18th century when French missionaries devised a way to render the spoken language using the Latin alphabet. Diacritical marks helped the reader to distinguish tones. In Vietnamese, the country's name is written Việt Nam. In English, the diacritical marks are dropped. Some texts, however, continue to write it Viet Nam or Viet-Nam. Others join the two words: Vietnam. American soldiers referred to it as "the 'Nam."

Rickshaws were a favored mode of transportation for French colonials in 19th-century Vietnam.

Similarly, in the 1920s the French introduced rubber cultivation to Vietnam, granting huge tracts of land to European owners. Rubber production boomed, but the benefits fell to Europeans. Labor conditions on the plantations were brutal and those who tried to leave were rounded up and, after due punishment, forced to complete their three-year contracts. In Vietnam, rubber was known as "white blood."

There was little support for French rule among the Vietnamese, even among those who benefited economically from the French presence. They had watched French taxes, land distribution, and government officials transform the country in ways that enriched France and impoverished the countryside. But repression kept open rebellion limited. Vietnamese intellectuals, many of them educated in schools established by the French as part of their "civilizing mission," debated among themselves about how best to achieve what all agreed was desirable: a unified, independent Vietnam. Many believed that would require Vietnam to transform itself into a modern, industrialized nation-state, on the model of France itself. Some favored fighting within the colonial system, to liberalize and eventually end it. Others argued for renewed, all-out resistance to expel the French altogether.

French colonial control of Indochina largely precluded American businesses and missionaries from working in that region, leaving the United States largely ignorant of the societies and peoples of Indochina. Despite the limited contact, the Vietnamese, in particular the intellectuals, knew far more about the United States that the other way around.

Ironically, given that years later the United States and Vietnam would be at war, many Vietnamese intellectuals found in the American revolution a source of inspiration for their own anti-colonialism. In the early 20th century, cheap biographies of America's founding fathers circulated widely within Vietnam, even after they were banned by French colonial authorities because of their "subversive" ideas. It was not only American history that appealed to the Vietnamese intellectuals, but also (despite U.S. annexation of the Philippines, among other territories) the declared opposition of the United States to European colonialism.

In 1919, President Woodrow Wilson identified the United States with the goal of self-determination for all nations, and during World War II President Franklin Delano Roosevelt was equally eloquent on the rights of colonial people to their independence. These messages gave hope to nationalists in colonized countries—including Vietnam's most famous anticolonial leader, Ho Chi Minh—that the United States might support their efforts to gain independence.

Nguyen That Thanh (Ho Chi Minh) was born in 1890, the son of a minor official who had himself fought against the French. Ho grew up listening to heroic tales of Vietnam's resistance to foreign domination, and while still a student at the National Academy in Hue, he participated in the short-lived anti-colonial movement of 1908. Then in 1911, like many Vietnamese intellectuals in the succeeding decades, Ho set off to see the world, taking odd jobs in a number of European and American cities.

Towards the end of World War I, Ho left London for Paris, where he worked in a photography shop and engaged in the vigorous intellectual and political life of the city. Taking the name Nguyen Ai Quoc (Nguyen the Patriot), Ho rose to prominence in

A French military officer with Vietnamese conscripts in 1913. The French recruited Vietnamese as early as 1879. During World War I, some 48,000 Vietnamese laborers were drafted for transport service in Europe; 25,000 were killed or wounded.

Vietnamese took a dim view of French social dancing, as this print illustrates: the name of the bar, "Nhay dam," means "jumping the woman" and is a pun on the Vietnamese word for animals copulating.

the Parisian Vietnamese community when he presented a petition to the peace conference meeting at Versailles in 1919 to end the war. Ho based his appeal for the expansion of Vietnamese political rights on the principle of self-determination declared by President Woodrow Wilson. But his petition was ignored by the conference and Ho began to search for some other path to independence.

In 1920, moved by the anti-colonial and anti-capitalist vision of the 1917 Russian revolution, Ho became a founding member of the French Communist Party. A few years later he was invited to Moscow to work with the Communist International (Comintern), whose task it was to encourage, train, and guide revolutionaries throughout the world. Then, meeting secretly with like-minded Vietnamese in Hong Kong in 1930, he established the Vietnamese Communist Party.

Over time, the Vietnamese resistance incorporated, and turned against the colonizers, the humanitarian ideas and emancipatory goals France claimed as its justification for the conquest of Vietnam, the very ideas the French taught Vietnamese in schools they established, the ideas embodied in the Declaration of the Rights of Man and the history of France's own great revolution. Those Vietnamese who sought both national independence and social reform drew inspiration from the German philosopher and revolutionary, Karl Marx, whose analysis of the political economy of capitalism and the potential for a more equitable socialist transformation of society was powerful and persuasive. From Vladimir Lenin, the founder of the Russian Communist Party, they learned the form of party organization, strategy, and tactics that had guided the Russian revolution of 1917. And in the Communist International (Comintern), established by the Soviet Union in 1919, Vietnamese revolutionaries found a source of direct material aid and support.

Communism, in the 1930s, seemed to hold the answer to the fundamental problems facing colonized people everywhere. The Soviet Union presented itself as a model for how a country might develop a modern industrial society and practice social justice at the same time. Its enemies, the capitalist colonial powers—France, Great Britain, the Netherlands, Germany, the United States— were also the enemies of Vietnamese, Chinese, Indians, Indonesians, Africans, and Filipinos struggling for independence, who gratefully accepted the advice of the world's first socialist country. However deeply Vietnamese and other colonized people admired America's own war of independence against Great Britain, or its democratic political system, however impressed they were with America's economic and, later, military power, a revolution led by a disciplined communist party seemed to many of them the only possible choice.

Throughout this period, Vietnamese continued to organize to free the country of French colonialism. Their task was complicated by World War II, when the Japanese seized Vietnam but retained the French administration. Now the Vietnamese had two colonial powers to defeat. There were many competing nationalist associations that sought support for their own efforts for Vietnamese independence from those countries fighting against Japan: the Vietnamese Nationalist Party (Viet Nam Quoc Dan Dan), for example, had close ties with Chiang Kai-shek and the Chinese Nationalists. But only one had a presence inside Vietnam itself and, with a little help from the United States, was able to train a small armed force: the Revolutionary League for the Independence of Vietnam (Doc Lap Dong Minh Hoi—generally known as the Viet Minh), an umbrella group led by the Vietnamese Communists under Ho Chi Minh.

Taking advantage of the Japanese defeat in August 1945, a defeat he hoped would mean the end of French colonialism as well, Ho Chi Minh announced the establishment of a provisional

Though sitting alone in my room, I shouted aloud as if addressing large crowds: "Dear martyrs, compatriots! This is what we need, this is what we need, this is the path to our liberation!"
—Ho Chi Minh describing his reaction in the 1920s to Vladimir Lenin's *Thesis on the National and Colonial Questions*

government of a "free Vietnam" and called for a general uprising against the Japanese-sponsored royal government throughout the country. Then, on Sept 2, 1945, acting as president of the provisional government, Ho declared Hanoi the capital of an independent, unified Democratic Republic of Vietnam (DRV).

The Vietnamese Declaration of Independence began with a direct quotation from what it called "the immortal statement" of the American revolution: "All men are created equal. They are endowed by their Creator with certain unalienable rights; among these are Life, Liberty and the pursuit of Happiness." The Declaration went on to list French abuses against the people of Vietnam. It was a very long list, starting with the deprivation of popular democratic rights and going on to charge that the French had built more prisons than schools; had robbed the country of its rice fields, mines, and forests; had destroyed national unity; and reduced the peasantry to extreme poverty. In short, "[the French] have acted contrary to the ideals of humanity and justice."

This promising beginning lasted less than a year. By 1946, the French, with the support of the United States, had returned to Vietnam in force, and war between France and the new republic had begun.

How did the United States come to fight in Vietnam? What path led America to oppose those Vietnamese who quoted its own Declaration of Independence?

The documents in this book trace the convoluted route that began on September 2, 1945, when Ho Chi Minh declared Vietnamese independence, to the moment, 30 years later, when the tanks of the Democratic Republic of Vietnam (North Vietnam) smashed the gates of the Presidential Palace in Saigon and reunited the country. Over those three decades there were many Vietnam wars: a war of independence against France, a civil war inside southern Vietnam, a civil war between South and North Vietnam, a war against the United States. Today, an independent Vietnam enjoys restored relations with the United States. Looking back, many people wonder why it took so much war to achieve this peace. Some of the answers lie in the documents. The following three documents illustrate both the diversity of Vietnamese nationalist thought and the role envisioned for the United States.

Evidence of the fascination with the American revolutionary war among Vietnamese intellectuals can be seen in the

writings of one of Vietnam's most prominent modern day nationalists: Phan Boi Chau, a scholar and activist, who had participated in the resistance to the French in the 1880s. Phan and his counterparts did not succeed in freeing Vietnam, nor did they live long enough to see the ultimate result of their efforts, but their examples were to fuel the passions of the next generation of committed Vietnamese nationalists.

This poem by Phan Boi Chau surveyed world history in an effort to teach particular lessons to the Vietnamese. It gives special attention to the role of George Washington in the American Revolution. Phan may have chosen to write about Washington because of his interpretation of one of the chief lessons of Washington's story: Vietnamese revolutionaries should attempt to infiltrate the French colonial militia to learn the tactics necessary to eventually overthrow French colonial rule in Vietnam.

Ho Chi Minh (far right) at the French Socialist Party Conference in 1920. Known then as Nguyen Ai Quoc ("Nugyen the Patriot"), Ho left the socialists for the newly formed French Communist Party, which he believed to be a stronger advocate of colonial independence.

Now we come to America or the United States
Where business is carried on in every profession
And there is great wealth on one hundred sides.
To develop the mind who do Americans rely upon?
They all rely upon [George] Washington;
Everyone relies upon the genius of Washington.
They tell the story of the time when as a young man he enlist-
 ed [in the British army],
At a time when the country felt humiliated because of the
 British presence.
He intended to quell this unpleasant situation
By uniting all the soldiers. For eight years he acted as he
 pleased;
Then he was able to fight and defeat the British.
Venerate Washington who served as commander-in-chief;
Follow the example of Washington who served as commander
 in-chief.

Although Ho Chi Minh was a communist for his entire adult life, he did not begin his public pursuit of resistance against the French as a communist. Ho Chi Minh, like his predecessors, hoped the capitalist United States would aid the Vietnamese in their search for independence. At the end of World War I, U.S. President Woodrow Wilson, speaking to

If you do not condemn colonialism, if you do not side with colonial people, what kind of revolution are you waging?

—Ho Chi Minh, describing in his 1960 book, *The Path Which Led Me to Leninism*, his debates with members of the French Communist Party

Congress, proclaimed his vision of a world that he hoped would emerge from the carnage of the war. U.S. policy would be devoted to "the principle of justice to all peoples and nationalities," Wilson promised, "and their right to live on equal terms of liberty and safety with one another." Ho took these statements to heart, and even though he had no official status, he nevertheless wrote a letter asking for American support for the ultimate self-determination of the people of Vietnam (Annamites). His letter, dated June 18, 1919, was addressed to Secretary of State Robert Lansing, Washington's representative at the Versailles Peace Conference. The Conference had been convened outside Paris in 1919 to settle the world's affairs in the aftermath of the war.

Ho's letter was clearly influenced by the U.S. Declaration of Independence and, no doubt, Ho thought that the similarities to that most formidable of American documents might have some effect on Lansing. It did not; there was no acknowledgment of the letter or Ho. In his appeal, Ho did not demand immediate independence from France, but rather an expansion of Vietnamese rights and participation in the French Parliament.

To his Excellency, the Secretary of State of the Republic of the United States, Delegate to the Peace Conference

Excellency,

We take the liberty of submitting to you the accompanying memorandum setting forth the claims of the Annamite people on the occasion of the Allied victory.

We count on your great kindness to honor our appeal by your support whenever the opportunity arises.

We beg your Excellency graciously to accept the expression of our profound respect.

For the Group of Annamite Patriots
[signed] Nguyen Ai Quoc
56, rue Monsieur le Prince, Paris

CLAIMS OF THE ANNAMITE PEOPLE

Since the victory of the Allies, all the subject peoples are frantic with hope at the prospect of an era of right and justice which should begin for them by virtue of the formal and solemn engagements, made before the whole world by the various powers of the entente in the struggle of civilization against barbarism.

While waiting for the principle of national self-determination to pass from ideal to reality through the effective recognition of the sacred right of all peoples to decide their own destiny, the inhabitants of the ancient Empire of Annam, at the present time French Indochina, present to the noble Governments of the entente in general and in particular to the honorable French Government the following humble claims:

(1) General amnesty for all the native people who have been condemned for political activity.

(2) Reform of Indochinese justice by granting to the native population the same judicial guarantees as the Europeans have, and the total suppression of the special courts which are the instruments of terrorization and oppression against the most responsible elements of the Annamite people.

(3) Freedom of press and speech.

(4) Freedom of association and assembly.

(5) Freedom to emigrate and to travel abroad.

(6) Freedom of education, and creation in every province of technical and professional schools for the native population.

(7) Replacement of the regime of arbitrary decrees by a regime of law.

(8) A permanent delegation of native people elected to attend the French parliament in order to keep the latter informed of their needs.

The Annamite people, in presenting these claims, count on the worldwide justice of all the Powers, and rely in particular on the goodwill of the noble French people who hold our destiny in their hands and who, as France is a republic, have taken us under their protection. In requesting the protection of the French people, the people of Annam, far from feeling humiliated, on the contrary consider themselves honored, because they know that the French people stand for liberty and justice and will never renounce their sublime ideal of universal brotherhood. Consequently, in giving heed to the voice of the oppressed, the French people will be doing their duty to France and to humanity.

In the Name of the Group of Annamite Patriots
Nguyen Ai Quoc

General Tran Van Don was also a nationalist, but an anti-communist. He was born and educated in France, joined the French Army during World War II, and rose to the rank of

lieutenant general in the French-sponsored Army of Vietnam. In the 1960s he was both a senator and member of the Vietnamese House of Representatives, as well as serving in various governments in Saigon, including as Minister of National Defense. In 1975, the day before Saigon fell to the communists, he left Vietnam for the United States. In his autobiography he described the nature of French rule and how it led him to his nationalist views.

As a schoolboy I learned that my ancient country had a rich tradition and desire to be independent. . . . France, in the second half of the nineteenth century, invaded Vietnam, transforming it into a colony. Her dominance lasted until after World War II, when Vietnam entered a new era. . . .

French influence had both positive and negative aspects. . . . The Vietnamese benefitted greatly from French advances in science and technology, health services, modern fishing methods, disease prevention, and the encouragement of industrial and business development. Our youth, including myself, learned of free enterprise and attended French schools, learned the French language, and came to realize that we could compete favorably with the Westerners in a variety of disciplines. As a by-product of all this education and example, many of us became political militants, prepared for the coming struggle against oppression. We learned from France herself, not the French colonialists, that we should fight to better the lot of the underprivileged and to recover independence and national unity.

Although we found much to admire in France as a nation and in French culture, we could never be content with the negative aspects of a colonial administration in Vietnam. The most remarkable attribute of this French political regime was that racial discrimination was practiced universally. . . . Many Vietnamese functionaries were better qualified to fill positions in the government than the Frenchmen who held them, but these locals were excluded. We were deprived of essential liberties by a prying, arbitrary police network which was aided by courts that systematically denied accused persons elementary rights of defense. . . .

A Vietnamese youth could go to France, spend five years there and graduate from a university with a first-class diploma only to find when he returned to Vietnam that he would be given a menial job, subordinate to the semiliterate Frenchman who had never completed high school.

French officers hold troop maneuvers in rice paddies in 1939. By 1940, the French colonial army in Indochina consisted of 20,000 Europeans, 40,000 North Africans from French colonies, and 60,000 Vietnamese. More than half of the Vietnamese deserted in the immediate aftermath of World War II. Many joined the Viet Minh.

Economic development always involved what benefitted France and her French colonists, not the Vietnamese. Vietnam was kept as dependent on the mother country as possible, but as a source of raw materials and as a captive market for French manufactured goods. . . .

In a few words, the people were fed up . . . nationalist sentiments and sub-rosa resistance were everywhere to be seen but failed to have any effect on the unseeing French.

Resistance to French rule was frequently not assessed for what it was, simple nationalist sentiment trying to achieve independence for our country. Shortly after the First World War, the French came to see our political opposition to the colonial regime as a manifestation of Communism. Some of our nationalist leaders, myself included, tried to work with the West towards Vietnamese independence. We were in a difficult position. To the French, and later the Americans, if we failed to agree with them we were either Communists or neutralists, while to the other side, by cooperating, we became puppets. . . .

I chose to follow the Western side while other equally patriotic Vietnamese took the Marxist path under the direction of Soviet Russia.

Chapter 1

The First Indochina War

Ho Chi Minh (center) arrives in
Paris to negotiate with the French in
1946. Earlier that year, the French
had agreed to give Vietnam control of
its internal affairs with a promise of
reunification in the near future. The
details were left vague, and the unilateral announcement by French
admiral Georges Thierry D'Argenlieu
establishing a separate Republic of
Cochin China cast doubt on the
entire agreement. Ho's expression was
appropriately gloomy.

In 1923, Ho Chi Minh became a member of the Communist
International (Comintern), whose goal was to promote, guide,
and support revolutionary activities throughout the world. For the
next decade he lived in exile, maintaining contact with both communist and noncommunist Vietnamese nationalists from Hong Kong
and southeast China. By the early 1940s Ho had established himself
fighting the Japanese in the mountainous border region between
Vietnam and China. It was here that he organized the Viet Nam Doc
Lap Dong Minh (League for Vietnamese Independence—the Viet
Minh), a broad coalition led by the Vietnamese Communist Party in
pursuit of a single goal: the independence of Vietnam.

After its surrender to Germany in 1940, France was divided
between a government that collaborated with the Germans (known, by
the name of its capitol, as Vichy France) and a zone occupied by the
Germans. Vichy France continued to administer Indochina throughout
the war—at first directly and then, after the Japanese invaded in 1941,
under close Japanese supervision. Thus, Ho Chi Minh and the United
States shared an enemy: the Japanese who occupied Vietnam. In the
fight against Japan, the United States found Ho Chi Minh's organization a useful ally, ready and willing to conduct guerilla raids on
Japanese forces, supply weather information as an aid to U.S. bombers,
and rescue airmen who had been shot down by the Japanese.

In March 1945, as the war in Europe came to a close, the Japanese
abruptly ended French colonial rule, disarmed French troops, arrested
French officials, and installed Bao Dai as heir to the Vietnamese
throne. As a result, when the war ended in August 1945 with the
unconditional surrender of Japan, the status of Indochina was unclear.
Defeat for Italy, Germany and Japan had meant the loss of their

VIET-NAM DAN CHU CONG HOA
—
CHINH PHU LAM THOI   HANOI FEBRUARY 28 1946

BO NGOAI GIAO
    *   TELEGRAM

PRESIDENT HOCHIMINH VIETNAM DEMOCRATIC REPUBLIC HANOI

TO THE PRESIDENT OF THE UNITED STATES OF AMERICA WASHINGTON D.C.

        ON BEHALF OF VIETNAM GOVERNMENT AND PEOPLE I BEG TO INFORM YOU

THAT IN COURSE OF CONVERSATIONS BETWEEN VIETNAM GOVERNMENT AND FRENCH

REPRESENTATIVES THE LATTER REQUIRE THE SECESSION OF COCHINCHINA AND THE

RETURN OF FRENCH TROOPS IN HANOI STOP MEANWHILE FRENCH POPULATION AND

TROOPS ARE MAKING ACTIVE PREPARATIONS FOR A COUP DE MAIN IN HANOI AND

FOR MILITARY AGGRESSION STOP I THEREFORE MOST EARNESTLY APPEAL TO YOU

PERSONALLY AND TO THE AMERICAN PEOPLE TO INTERFERE URGENTLY IN SUPPORT

OF OUR INDEPENDENCE AND HELP MAKING THE NEGOTIATIONS MORE IN KEEPING WITH

THE PRINCIPLES OF THE ATLANTIC AND SAN FRANCISCO CHARTERS

    RESPECTFULLY

                                        HOCHIMINH

One of several letters of appeal written by Ho Chi Minh to President Harry S. Truman in 1945 and 1946. There was no response.

colonies. But what of France? In London, General Charles De Gaulle had organized a government in exile and a fighting force, the Free French, which opposed the Vichy government and allied itself with the United States, Great Britain, and the Soviet Union. Now, in 1945, a restored French Republic demanded the restoration of its colonies. Just as India remained British, so should Indochina remain French.

President Franklin D. Roosevelt, whose disapproval of French colonial policy was well known, urged trusteeship under the supervision of the newly organized United Nations, but this idea died with Roosevelt in April 1945. American policy toward Vietnam would be shaped instead by how U.S. leaders understood the postwar world.

In the immediate postwar period, the United States focused first on the revitalization of Europe. The need for strong allies there shaped initial American responses to French efforts to reinstall its colonial control over Indochina. Despite efforts by Ho Chi Minh to come to some compromise agreement with the French, war broke out in Vietnam between the French and Vietnamese in 1946. With some reluctance, the U.S. supported France, at first indirectly; by 1950 it had assumed virtually all of the costs of the French war—$1.1 billion in 1954 alone. The end of the Chinese civil war in 1949 with a victory for the Chinese Communist Party gave Ho Chi Minh a powerful ally in the struggle against the French. To U.S. policymakers, the Chinese Communist victory made support for France more imperative than ever.

On September 2, 1945, Ho Chi Minh and his Viet Minh forces marched into Hanoi where Ho, before a huge audience which included members of the American Office of Strategic Services (OSS), forerunner of the Central Intelligence Agency (CIA), declared the independence of the Democratic Republic of Vietnam. As he composed his speech, Ho checked with his American friends in the OSS for the exact wording of the Declaration of Independence. The speech also drew from the French Declaration of the Rights of Man and of the Citizen.

But its main thrust was a lengthy indictment of the French record in Vietnam.

All men are created equal. They are endowed by their Creator with certain unalienable Rights: among these are Life, Liberty, and the pursuit of Happiness.

This immortal statement was made in the Declaration of Independence of the United States of America in 1776. In a broader sense, this means: All the peoples on the earth are equal from birth, all the peoples have a right to live, to be happy and free.

The Declaration of the French Revolution made in 1791 on the Rights of Man and the Citizen also states: "All men are born free and with equal rights, and must always remain free and have equal rights."

These are undeniable truths.

An editorial cartoon by J. Costello expresses dissatisfaction with U.S. funding of the French war and the lack of gratitude expressed by the French.

Nevertheless, for more than eighty years, the French imperialists, abusing the principles of Freedom, Equality, and Fraternity, have violated our Fatherland and oppressed our fellow-citizens. They have acted contrary to the ideals of humanity and justice.

In the field of politics, they have deprived our people of every democratic liberty. They have enforced inhuman laws; they have set up three distinct political regimes in the North, the Center and the South of Vietnam in order to wreck our national unity and prevent our people from being united.

They have built more prisons than schools. They have mercilessly slain our patriots; they have drowned our uprisings in rivers of blood.

They have fettered public opinion; they have practiced obscurantism against our people.

To weaken our race they have forced us to use opium and alcohol.

In the field of economics, they have fleeced us to the backbone, impoverished our people, and devastated our land. They have robbed us of our rice fields, our mines, our forests, and our raw materials. They have monopolized the issuing of bank-notes and the export trade. They have invented numerous unjustifiable taxes and reduced our people, especially our peasantry, to a state of extreme poverty.

They have hampered the prospering of our national bourgeoisie; they have mercilessly exploited our workers.

After the Japanese had surrendered to the Allies, our whole people rose to regain our national sovereignty and to found the Democratic Republic of Vietnam. . . . We, members of the Provisional Government, representing the whole Vietnamese people, declare that from now on we break off all relations of a colonial character with France; we repeal all the international obligation that France has so far subscribed to on behalf of Vietnam and we abolish all the special rights the French have unlawfully acquired in our Fatherland.

The whole Vietnamese people, animated by a common purpose, are determined to fight to the bitter end against any attempt by the French colonialists to reconquer their country. . . .

We, members of the Provisional Government of the Democratic Republic of Vietnam, solemnly declare to the world that Vietnam has the right to be a free and independent country—and in fact is so already. The entire Vietnamese people are determined to mobilize all their physical and mental strength, to

sacrifice their lives and property in order to safeguard their independence and liberty.

Vo Nguyen Giap (left, in derby hat) reviews Viet Minh troops. Poorly armed and barely trained, these troops nevertheless managed to control much of the countryside, confining the French to the cities.

Vietnam Approaches America

From 1940 to 1945, Ho had two objectives: to defeat the Japanese military and to secure Vietnam's freedom from France. He hoped the United States would help him with both objectives. At the same time, he recognized that the claims of small nations such as his own might not weigh very heavily in postwar power considerations. On August 6, 1945, he expressed both his hopes and his fears in a private letter to one of his OSS liaison officers, Charles Fenn. Although Ho spoke some English, he was not fluent, and the text here is an exact reproduction of what he wrote, mistakes and all.

The war is finished. It is good for everybody. I feel only sorry that all our American friends have to leave us so soon. And their leaving this country means that relations between you and us will be more difficult.

The war is won. But we small and subject countries have no share, or very small share, in the victory of freedom and democracy.

Postage stamp of His Majesty Bao Dai, emperor from 1925 until his abdication in 1945. Bao Dai became emperor once again when the French returned him to nominal power in 1949. When Diem took power in 1955, Bao Dai was exiled to France.

Probably, if we want to get a sufficient share, we have still to fight. I believe that your sympaty and the sympaty of the great American will always be with us.

I also remain sure that sooner or later, we will attain our aim, because it is just. And our country get independent. I am looking forward for the happy day of meeting you and our other American friends either in Indo-China or in the USA!

I wish you good luck & good health.

In addition to writing to his friends, Ho also wrote some eight letters to President Harry S. Truman, appealing for American support against the French. Ho held some hope that despite his communist affiliations, the United States might still be willing to stand by his anticolonial rhetoric. This is one such letter. Ho refers here to the granting of independence to the Philippines by the United States on July 4, 1946.

16 February 1946

I avail myself of this opportunity to thank you and the people of United States for the interest shown by your representatives at the United Nations Organization in favour of the dependent peoples.

Our VIETNAM people, as early as 1941, stood by the Allies' side and fought against the Japanese and their associates, the French colonialists.

From 1941 to 1945 we fought bitterly, sustained by the patriotism of our fellow-countrymen and by the promises made by the Allies at [the summits in] YALTA, SAN FRANCISCO AND POTSDAM.

When the Japanese were defeated in August 1945, the whole Vietnam territory was united under a Provisional Republican Government which immediately set out to work. In five months, peace and order were restored, a democratic republic was established on legal basis and adequate help was given to the Allies in the carrying out of their disarmament mission.

But the French colonialists, who had betrayed in war-time both the Allies and the Vietnamese, have come back and are waging on us a murderous and pitiless war in order to reestablish their domination. . . .

This aggression is contrary to all principles of international law and to the pledges made by the Allies during the World War. It is a challenge to the noble attitude shown before, during and after the war by the United States Government and People. It violently contrasts with the firm stand you have taken in your twelve point [January 1, 1942, United Nations] declaration, and with the idealistic loftiness and generosity expressed by your delegates to the United Nations Assembly. . . .

The French aggression on a peace-loving people is a direct menace to world security. It implies the complicity, or at least, the connivance of the Great Democracies. The United Nations ought to keep their word. They ought to interfere to stop this unjust war, and to show that they mean to carry out in peace-time the principles for which they fought in war-time. . . .

It is with this firm conviction that we request of the United States as guardians and champions of World Justice to take a decisive step in support of our independence.

What we ask has been graciously granted to the Philippines. Like the Philippines our goal is full independence and full cooperation with the UNITED STATES. We will do our best to make this independence and cooperation profitable to the whole world.

I am, dear Mr. PRESIDENT,
Respectfully Yours,
Ho Chi Minh

America Responds

Within the U.S. government there was considerable disagreement over whether to cooperate with Ho; was he a communist first or a nationalist above all else? The former view won out, and in September 1948 the Department of State expressed the official U.S. policy toward Indochina—the French term for Laos, Cambodia, and Vietnam—in its first full-length statement on the region. From Woodrow Wilson's Fourteen Points through the 1940 Atlantic Charter, the United States had always declared itself in favor of the right of self-determination for all people. Thus, full support of military reconquest by the French was ruled out as going against American principles.

However, the State Department also opposed French military withdrawal on the grounds that it would lead to "chaos and terroristic activities." The difficulty for the United States was twofold: First, its commitment to Western Europe entailed a strong French ally in the unfolding Cold War. France could not be allowed to drain its resources in an endless colonial war, nor could the United States afford to alienate the French by opposing French sovereignty in Indochina. Secondly, though the United States recognized the force of national-

Bao Dai's Declaration of Abdication

In August 1945, Bao Dai, who had served as Vietnamese emperor in the Japanese-organized government, abdicated the throne and briefly worked in the new government organized by Ho Chi Minh. But as war between France and Vietnam developed, Bao Dai resigned in favor of his more usual haunts along the French Riviera. His declaration of abdication may be one of his few acts of genuine nationalism.

THE HAPPINESS OF THE PEOPLE OF VIETNAM. THE INDEPENDENCE OF VIETNAM. To achieve these ends, we have declared ourself ready for any sacrifice and we desire that our sacrifice be useful to the people. . . .

We have decided to abdicate and we transer power to the democratic Republican Government. . . .

As for us, during twenty years' reign, we have known much bitterness. Henceforth, we shall be happy to be a free citizen of an independent country. We shall allow no one to abuse our name or the name of the royal family in order to sow dissent among our compatriots.

Long live the independence of Vietnam!
Long live our Democratic Republic!

A French Foreign Legion patrol flushes
a suspect from his hiding place in the
jungle. The Foreign Legion had first
fought against Vietnamese in 1883, and
it remained a mainstay of French military presence in Indochina until 1953.

**ism in Asia, it steadfastly refused to sanction any commu-
nist-led insurgency, however popular. Efforts to find a suitable nationalist replacement for Ho Chi Minh and at the
same time persuade the French to grant some form of independence to Vietnam remained constants of U.S. policy from
this time forward. These contradictory elements are reflected in the following State Department review of policy.**

A. Objectives

The immediate objective of U.S. policy in Indochina is to assist in
a solution of the present impasse which will be mutually satisfactory to the French and the Vietnamese peoples, which will result
in the termination of the present hostilities, and which will be
within the framework of U.S. security.

Our long-term objectives are: (1) to eliminate so far as possible Communist influence in Indochina and to see installed a self-
governing nationalist state which will be friendly to the US . . . ;
(2) to foster the association of the peoples of Indochina with the
western powers, particularly with France with whose customs, language and laws they are familiar . . . ; (3) to raise the standard of
living so that the peoples of Indochina will be less receptive to
totalitarian influences . . . ; (4) to prevent undue Chinese penetra-
tion and subsequent influence in Indochina so that the peoples of
Indochina will not be hampered in their natural developments by
the pressure of an alien people and alien interests.

B. Policy Issues

To attain our immediate objective, we should continue to press
the French to accommodate the basic aspirations of the
Vietnamese: (1) unity of Cochinchina, Annam, and Tonkin, (2)
complete internal autonomy, and (3) the right to choose freely
regarding participation in the French Union. We have recognized
French sovereignty over Indochina but have maintained that such
recognition does not imply any commitment on our part to assist
France to exert its authority over the Indochinese peoples. Since
V-J day, the majority people of the area, the Vietnamese, have
stubbornly resisted the reestablishment of French authority, a
struggle in which we have tried to maintain insofar as possible a
position of non-support of either party.

While the nationalist movement in Vietnam . . . is strong, and
though the great majority of the Vietnamese are not fundamen-
tally Communist, the most active element in the resistance of the
local peoples to the French has been a Communist group headed
by Ho Chi Minh. This group has successfully extended its influ-

ence to include practically all armed forces now fighting the French, thus in effect capturing control of the nationalist movement. . . . Since early in 1947, the French have employed about 115,000 troops in Indochina, with little result, since the countryside . . . remains under the firm control of the Ho Chi Minh government. A series of French-established puppet governments have tended to enhance the prestige of Ho's government and to call into question . . . the sincerity of French intentions to accord an independent status to Vietnam.

C. Political
We have regarded these hostilities in a colonial area as detrimental not only to our own long-term interests which require as a minimum a stable Southeast Asia but also detrimental to the interest of France, since the hatred engendered by continuing hostilities may render impossible peaceful collaboration and cooperation of the French and the Vietnamese peoples. This hatred of the Vietnamese people toward the French is keeping alive anti-western feeling among oriental peoples, to the advantage of the USSR and the detriment of the US. We have not urged the French to negotiate with Ho Chi Minh, even though he probably is now supported by a considerable majority of the Vietnamese people, because of his record as a Communist and the Communist background of many of the influential figures in and about his government. . . .

In accord with our policy of regarding with favor the efforts of dependent peoples to attain their legitimate political aspirations, we have been anxious to see the French accord to the Vietnamese the largest possible degree of political and economic independence consistent with legitimate French interests. . . .

D. Policy Evaluation
The objectives of US policy towards Indochina have not been realized. . . . The objectives of US policy can only be attained by such French action as will satisfy the nationalist aspirations of the peoples of Indochina. We have repeatedly pointed out to the French the desirability of their giving such satisfaction and thus terminating the present open conflict. Our greatest difficulty in talking with the French and in stressing what should and what should not be done has been our inability to suggest any practicable solution of the Indochina problem, as we are all too well aware of the unpleasant fact that Communist Ho Chi Minh is the strongest and perhaps the ablest figure in Indochina and that any suggested solution which excluded him is an expedient of uncertain outcome. . . . The above considerations are further com-

Viet Minh forces enter Hanoi in 1954. After eight years of fighting, the possibility of peace and reunification animated both the troops and the crowd.

plicated by the fact that we have an immediate interest in maintaining in power a friendly French Government, to assist in the furtherance of our aims in Europe. This immediate and vital interest has in consequence taken precedence over active steps looking toward the realization of our objectives in Indochina.

Not everyone in the government of the United States agreed with the official policy, nor with the view of America's role as the arbitrator of what form of government other nations should have. Writing in his memoirs, one of the foremost American diplomats of that period, George Kennan, recalled his efforts to urge a more cautious policy in Asia.

There remains the question of Southeast Asia. This, too, was on our minds, even in 1950 and 1951 though primarily in connection with the question as to the amount of support, if any, that we should give to the French, who were then fighting much the same sort of fight, and against much the same adversary that we, in the years following 1964, found ourselves fighting. . . .

We had, I felt, no business trying to play a role in the affairs of the mainland of Southeast Asia. The same went for the French. They had no prospects. They had better get out. "In Indo-China," I complained to the Secretary of State in the memo of August 21, 1950,

> . . . we are getting ourselves into the position of guarantee-ing the French in an undertaking which neither they nor we, nor both of us together, can win. . . . We should let Schuman [Robert Schuman, French Foreign Minister] know . . . that the closer view we have had of the problems of this area, in the course of our efforts of the past few months to support the French position there, has convinced us that that posi-tion is basically hopeless. We should say that we will do everything in our power to avoid embarrassing the French in their problems and to support them in any reasonable course they would like to adopt looking to its liquidation; but that we cannot honestly agree with them that there is any real hope of their remaining successfully in Indo-China, and we feel that rather than have their weakness demonstrated by a continued costly and unsuccessful effort to assert their will by force of arms, it would be preferable to permit the turbu-lent political currents of that country to find their own level, unimpeded by foreign troops or pressures, even at the prob-able cost of an eventual deal between Viet-Nam and Viet-Minh, and the spreading over the whole country of Viet-Minh authority, possibly in a somewhat modified form. . . .

This judgment with regard to the folly of a possible intervention in Vietnam rested, incidentally, not just on the specific aspects of that situation as we faced it in 1950, but on considerations of prin-ciple, as well. In a lecture delivered earlier that year (May 5) in Milwaukee, I had said—this time with reference to the pleas for American intervention in China:

> I wonder how many of you realize what that really means. I can conceive of no more ghastly and fateful mistake, and nothing more calculated to confuse the issues in this world today than for us to go into another great country and try to uphold by force of our own blood and treasures a regime which had clearly lost the confidence of its own people. Nothing could have pleased our enemies more. . . . Had our Government been carried away by these pressures . . . I am

In Indo-China, we are getting ourselves into the position of guaranteeing the French in any undertaking which neither they nor we, nor both of us together can win.

—State Department official George Kennan in a memo to Secretary of State Dean Acheson, August 21, 1950

confident that today the whole struggle against world communism in both Europe and Asia would have been hopelessly fouled up and compromised.

Little did I realize, in penning these passages, that I was defining, fifteen years before the event, my own position with relation to the Vietnam War.

During the Cold War, American and Soviet policymakers viewed the world in terms of a zero-sum game; that is, a winner and a loser, no ties. Countries had to choose sides, and there was very little tolerance for those not willing to align themselves completely with either side. Which side was Ho Chi Minh on? In his telegram to the U.S. Consulate in Hanoi on May 29, 1949, Secretary of State Dean Acheson gives instructions, in the language designed for telegrams, on how to decide. Acheson's conviction that "all Stalinists in colonial areas are nationalists," made the question of Ho's deepest allegiances effectively irrelevant to U.S. policymakers.

In light Ho's known background, no other assumption possible but that he outright Commie so long as (1) he fails unequivocally to repudiate Moscow connections and Commie doctrine and (2) remains personally singled out for praise by international Commie press and receives its support. Moreover, US not impressed by nationalist character red flag with yellow stars. Question whether Ho as much nationalist as Commie is irrelevant. All Stalinists in colonial areas are nationalists. With achievement national aims (i.e., independence) their objective necessarily becomes subordination state to Commie purposes and ruthless extermination not only opposition groups but all elements suspected even slightest deviation. On basis examples eastern Europe it must be assumed such would be goal Ho and men his stamp. . . . To include them in order to achieve reconciliation opposing political elements and "national unity" would merely postpone settlement issue whether Vietnam to be independent nation or Commie satellite until circumstances probably even less favorable nationalists than now. It must of course be conceded theoretical possibility exists establish National Communist state on pattern Yugoslavia in any area beyond reach Soviet army. However, US attitude could take account such possibility only if every other possible avenue closed to preservation area from Kremlin control. Moreover, while Vietnam out of reach Soviet army it will doubtless be by no means out of reach Chi Commie hatchet men and armed forces.

As the Cold War deepened, the policies of the United States toward any allies of the Soviet Union hardened. In Indochina the United States moved quickly from trying to prevent war between France and Vietnam to funding the French war effort, believing that only a communist defeat would be a suitable solution for Indochina. As the war dragged on without a French victory, the French public began to turn against it, complaining of drained resources and growing combat deaths. To alleviate the French burden, the United States began paying for the war. By 1954 Washington was responsible for some 80 percent of the cost of the war and the United States, unbeknownst to most Americans, was now deeply engaged in Southeast Asia. With French defeat in Indochina imminent, President Dwight D. Eisenhower explained at a press conference why Vietnam was a matter of direct importance to the United States.

ROBERT RICHARDS, COPLEY PRESS: Mr. President, would you mind commenting on the strategic importance of Indochina to the free world? I think there has been, across the country, some lack of understanding of just what it means to us.

THE PRESIDENT: You have, of course, both the specific and the general when you talk about such things.

First of all, you have the specific value of a locality in its production of materials that the world needs. Then you have the possibility that many human beings pass under a dictatorship that is inimical to the free world. Finally, you have broader considerations that might follow what you would call the "falling domino" principle. You have a row of dominoes set up, you knock over the first one, and what will happen to the last one is the certainty that it will go over very quickly. So you could have a beginning of a disintegration that would have the most profound influences.

Now, with respect to the first one, two of the items from this particular area that the world uses are tin and tungsten. They are very important. There are others, of course, the rubber plantations and so on.

Then with respect to more people passing under this domination, Asia, after all, has already lost some 450 million of its peoples to the Communist dictatorship, and we simply can't afford greater losses.

"How about the other buttons?" This cartoon reflects the common U.S. view that the Soviet Union pushed the buttons responsible for unrest in countries from Korea and Indochina to Yugoslavia.

But when we come to the possible sequence of events, the loss of Indochina, of Burma, of Thailand, of the Peninsula, and Indonesia following, now you begin to talk about areas that not only multiply the disadvantages that you would suffer through loss of sources of materials, but now you are talking really about millions and millions and millions of people.

Finally, the geographical position achieved thereby does many things. It turns the so-called island defensive chain of Japan, Formosa, of the Philippines and to the southward; it moves in to threaten Australia and New Zealand.

It takes away, in its economic aspects, that region that Japan must have as a trading area or Japan, in turn, will have only one place in the world to go—that is, toward the Communist areas in order to live.

So, the possible consequences of the loss are just incalculable to the free world.

Only days after President Eisenhower's comments, his Vice President, Richard M. Nixon, spoke to a reporter on condition that he not be named. In this talk, which was at times remarkably prescient, Nixon said openly what Eisenhower administration officials may have been thinking but had not said so blatantly in public.

The official remarked that "the United States, as the leader of the free world, cannot afford further retreat in Asia." He expressed the view that the Communist forces could be stopped "without American boys," but added, "we must take the risk of putting American boys in the fighting," if there is no other way. . . .

Among the statements he made were these:

The situation in Southeast Asia is currently the most important issue facing the United States. It relates to a war we might have to fight and that we might lose. . . .

From the Communist point of view the war in Korea is about Japan, he continued, and so is the war in Indo-China which is essential to Japan's economic survival. Without trade with Indochina and Korea and with these countries under Communist control, Japan would become an economic satellite of the Soviet Union. . . .

But he saw no reason why the French forces should not win in Indo-China. . . . the problem is not materials but men, he said and they will not come from France which is tired of the war; they must come from Vietnam, Cambodia, and Laos. But the French

CH XƠN   GIÔN XƠN   KEN NƠ ĐI   AI XEN HAO

have been slow in training the native soldiers.

Even more difficult is the problem of giving the Indo-Chinese the will to fight, he said. He took issue with the view that if the French got out, the Indo-Chinese would fight to keep their independence, saying Indo-China would be Communist-dominated within a month if the French left.

So the United States must . . . take a positive stand for united action by the free world, he asserted, or it will have to take on the problem alone and try to sell it to the others. There will be French pressure . . . to negotiate and the end the fighting at any cost, he said, and the British position will be somewhat similar because of mounting Labor Party pressure and defections in the Conservative ranks. The British do not want to antagonize Red China, which they have recognized.

This country is the only country that is strong enough politically at home to take a position that will save Asia, the official continued. . . .

But, with or without the support of public opinion, if the situation in Indo-China requires that American troops be sent there to prevent that area from disappearing behind the Iron Curtain, the Administration must face the issue and send the troops, he declared.

The involvement Nixon anticipated in late 1953 is caricatured in this Vietnamese cartoon from the early 1970s. From left, the Presidents shown are Richard Nixon, Lyndon B. Johnson, John F. Kennedy, and Dwight D. Eisenhower. The caption to this cartoon read "The 'traditional burden' of American presidents" and reflected the North Vietnamese view of American involvement in the war.

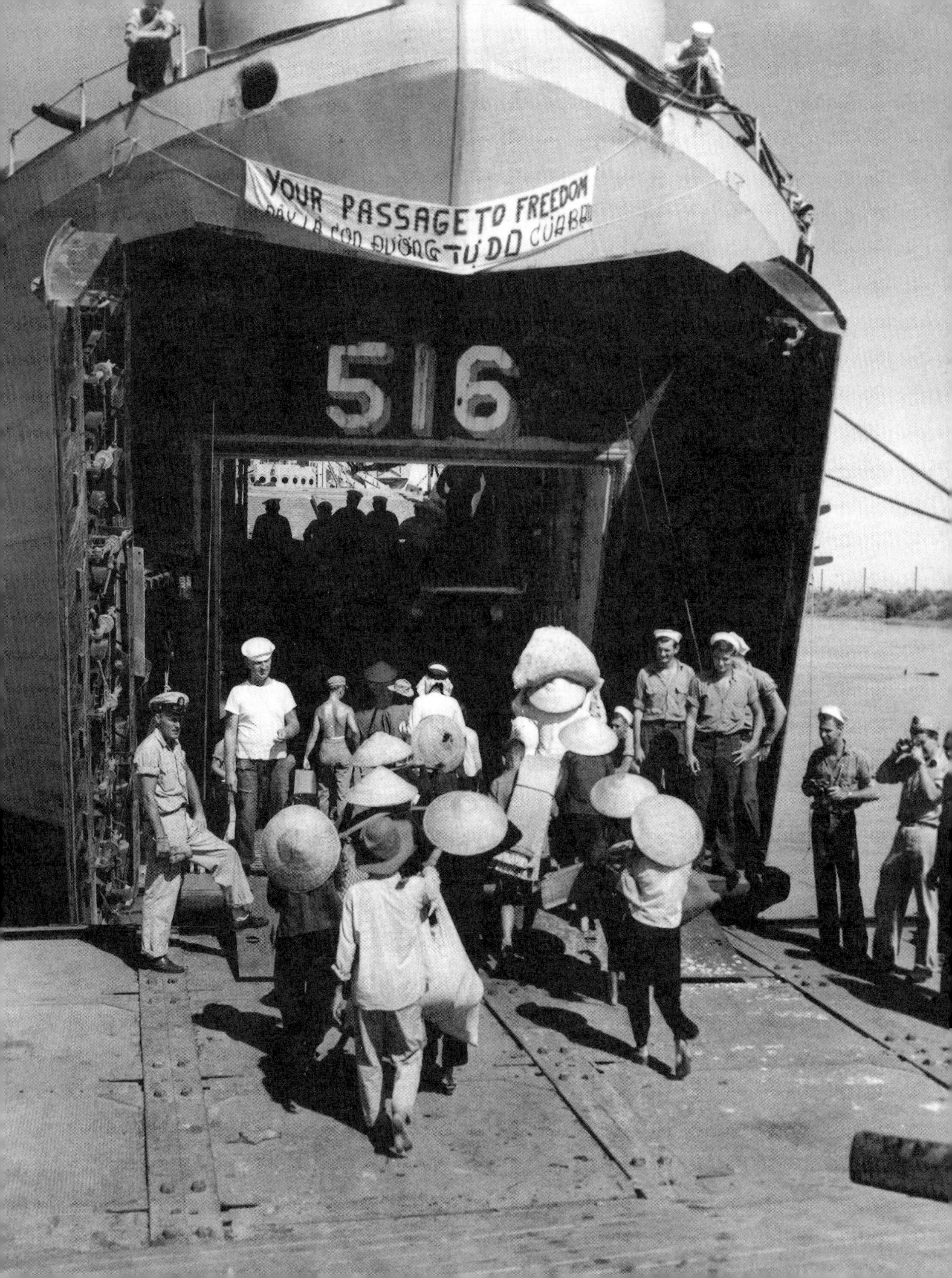
YOUR PASSAGE TO FREEDOM
LÀ CON ĐƯỜNG TỰ DO CỦA
516

Chapter 2

Waist Deep in the Big Muddy

Despite substantial U.S. financial assistance and years of brutal warfare, the French government was unable to achieve its aims in Vietnam. In May 1954 the Viet Minh overran the French garrison at Dien Bien Phu to bring an effective end to French rule in Vietnam. A conference that had been called in Geneva to deal with lingering issues of the Korean War and the status of Berlin, would now deal with Vietnam as well. Delegates from the People's Republic of China, France, the Soviet Union, and Great Britain were joined in May by representatives from Laos, Cambodia, and the two competing governments of a single Vietnamese state: the Democratic Republic of Vietnam (recognized by the Soviet Union and the People's Republic of China in 1950) and the State of Vietnam (created by the French in 1950, who recalled former emperor Bao Dai to the throne, and recognized by the U.S. and its allies).

The political struggle in Geneva continued until July, when a final proclamation was signed by all of the participants except the United States and the U.S.-sponsored government of the State of Vietnam. The accord called for universal recognition of Ho Chi Minh's government in Hanoi, an end to the fighting, the withdrawal of foreign forces from Vietnam, the temporary partition of the country into two zones at the 17th parallel: the Democratic Republic of Vietnam to the north of the line, the State of Vietnam to the south. An internationally supervised nationwide election to unify the country would be held in 1956.

Waist Deep in the Big Muddy

The title of this chapter comes from a song written in the 1960s by folksinger and political activist, Pete Seeger. The song itself is, on the face of it, a simple story of the difficulties encountered in 1942 by a World War II training platoon whose men risk death crossing a swollen stream in Louisiana. The last four lines, "Every time I read the papers/ That old feeling comes on/ We're waist deep in the Big Muddy/ And the big fool says to push on" were meant, however, to be a criticism of the American war in Vietnam. In 1967, CBS-TV executives forbade him from singing the song on television.

Not everyone was happy with the final declaration. The Viet Minh, having achieved victory on the battlefield, were especially disturbed at having to accept a partition of their country—even if only for two years—and did so under pressure from their Chinese and Russian allies. Both Moscow and Beijing were anxious to resolve the Vietnamese situation, seeing it as an obstacle to their efforts to better relations with the noncommunist world, especially the United States and Western Europe.

Emperor Bao Dai, under pressure from Washington and a group of influential Americans, organized as the American Friends of Vietnam, appointed Ngo Dinh Diem prime minister in June 1954. A devout Catholic (one of his brothers, Ngo Dinh Thuc, was the Archbishop of Hue), Diem was both an anti-French and anti-Communist nationalist. Through his political and religious affiliations Diem was well known to various American religious and political leaders, who championed him as their preferred Vietnamese leader. In July 1954 he returned to Vietnam from his voluntary exile at a Catholic seminary in New Jersey. From this moment until his overthrow in 1963, American policy was closely linked to his success or failure.

Ngo Dinh Diem was born in 1901 to a family that had converted to Catholicism from Buddhism centuries earlier. His father was a high court official and Diem himself received a French seminary education and worked his way up the civil service ranks. He might have served in the "independent" government Japan had set up in March 1945, but before negotiations could be completed, Japan surrendered. Diem's anticommunism was reinforced after the execution of his brother, a provincial governor, by the Viet Minh, and he spurned an offer from Ho Chi Minh to join his government. By 1955, after a rocky start, Diem managed to consolidate his control over the government in Saigon. But Diem turned out to be a far less successful leader than Washington and his private supporters had hoped. He had some built-in disadvantages as a Catholic in a predominantly Buddhist country. Yet he did little to overcome this obstacle. He was a man committed, above all else and at any cost, to maintaining his rule. He crushed any opposition to his government and with the help of his extended family—especially his brother-in-law, Ngo Dinh Nhu, who served as his chief political advisor and head of the secret police—created a dictatorial regime in the South.

Diem's policies were hardly designed to enhance his popularity. For example, in 1956 his government abolished elected village councils and replaced them with officials who were appointed by

Diem based solely on their loyalty to him. Diem also alienated Buddhists, who made up some 85 percent of the Vietnamese population, by appointing Catholics to official government and military office based on their religious affiliation. And he did nothing to win the trust of the peasants who made up the majority of the populace. In early 1957 Diem, under pressure from the United States, instituted a land reform designed to end absentee landlordism, but because absentee landlords were a vital source of political support for Diem, the program was never seriously implemented. Nor did he win the affections of an important middle class of ethnic Chinese, living mostly in the area of Saigon called Cholon. Instead,

On a visit to New York in 1957, Ngo Dinh Diem paid his respects to Bishop Joseph F. Flannelly, one of his many American admirers.

he passed laws forbidding foreign ownership of retail businesses. Although most Chinese managed to retain control of their enterprises by becoming Vietnamese citizens or enlisting Vietnamese partners, Diem had alienated a group that might have provided important economic and political support in times of need.

Diem was now left with only one significant source of opposition. There were about 10,000 Viet Minh left in southern Vietnam after most of their comrades had moved north to comply with the Geneva Accords. Diem disdainfully referred to them as Viet Cong; the equivalent English term would be "Vietnamese Commies." Diem ordered mass arrests of anyone suspected of harboring anti-Diem sentiments. Of the 100,000 people subsequently arrested, many were tortured and thousands were executed.

The Viet Minh survivors pleaded with Hanoi to authorize armed struggle against Diem, but were told that, for the moment, opposition to Diem must remain entirely political. The north was still recovering from the consequences of the war against France. In 1957 the surviving members of the Viet Minh in the south did launch a campaign of assassination against absentee landlords and the most oppressive of Diem's rural officials. Diem's response was to establish the Agroville Program, the name referring to the new villages into which peasants were forced to move, far from their homes and ancestral graves. Enclosed by barbed wire, more prison camp than village, the Agrovilles were intended to separate peasants from any contact with communist insurgents.

Hanoi had hoped that the struggle in the south could be carried out mainly by political means but in 1959 the policy changed and political organizers began to infiltrate south, especially native southerners who had moved north in 1954. Their role was to begin to organize armed resistance to Diem's government.

A Temporary Peace

The Final Declaration of the Geneva Conference, issued on July 21, 1954, did not satisfy everyone but it did reach important points of agreement that allowed for a military cease-fire and the possibility of a more permanent peace. Supervision of the cease-fire and the elections, which were intended to unify the country, was vested in the International Control Commission (ICC), whose member countries had not been involved in the war on either side: Canada, India, and Poland. However, the ICC had no power to enforce its recommendations. Its members were only rarely in agreement, and its reports of violations by all parties to the agreement were ignored except as they served the propaganda needs of the contending groups. Here are excerpts of the main points of the Final Declaration.

1. The Conference takes note of the Agreements ending hostilities in Cambodia, Laos, and Vietnam and organizing international control and the supervision of the execution of the provisions of these agreements. . . .

4. The Conference takes note of the clauses in the Agreement on the cessation of hostilities in Vietnam prohibiting the introduction into Vietnam of foreign troops and military personnel as well as all kinds of arms and munitions. . . .

6. The Conference recognizes that the essential purpose of the Agreement is to settle military questions with a view to ending hostilities and that the military demarcation line is provisional and should not in any way be interpreted as constituting a political or territorial boundary. . . .

7. The Conference declares that, so far as Vietnam is concerned, the settlement of political problems, effected on the basis of respect for principles of independence, unity and territorial integrity, shall permit the Vietnamese people to enjoy the fundamental freedoms, guaranteed by democratic institutions established as a result of free general elections by secret ballot

The opening of the Geneva Conference, April 17, 1954. Numbers identify the key delegates: (1) George Bidault, premier of France, (2) John Foster Dulles, U.S. secretary of state, (3) Anthony Eden, British foreign secretary, (4) Zhou Enlai, premier, People's Republic of China, and (5) General Nam Il, North Korea.

. . . , general elections shall be held in July 1956, under the supervision of an international commission composed of representatives of the Member States of the International Supervisory Commission. . . .

8. The provisions of the Agreements on the cessation of hostilities intended to ensure the protection of individuals and of property must be most strictly applied and must, in particular, allow everyone in Vietnam to decide freely in which zone he wishes to live.

9. The competent representative authorities of the Northern and Southern zones of Viet-Nam, as well as the authorities of Laos and Cambodia, must not permit any individual or collective reprisals against persons who have collaborated in any way with one of the parties during the war, or against members of such persons' families.

10. The Conference takes note of the declaration of the Government of the French Republic to the effect that it is ready to withdraw its troops from the territory of Cambodia, Laos and Vietnam. . . .

12. In their relations with Cambodia, Laos and Vietnam, each member of the Geneva Conference undertakes to respect the sovereignty, the independence, the unity and the territorial integrity of the above-mentioned States, and to refrain from any interference in their internal affairs.

Washington was unhappy about the recognition of a communist government in Hanoi and refused to sign the final agreement. The U.S. delegate to the Geneva Conference, Walter Bedell Smith, offered the following response.

The Government of the United States being resolved to devote its efforts to the strengthening of peace in accordance with the principles and purposes of the United States takes note of the agreements concluded at Geneva on July 20 and 21, 1954. . . . [The U.S.] declares with regard to the aforesaid agreements and paragraphs that (i) it will refrain from the threat or the use of force to disturb them. . . ; and (ii) it would view any renewal of the aggression in violation of the aforesaid agreements with grave concern and as seriously threatening international peace and security.

In the case of nations now divided against their will, we shall continue to seek to achieve unity through free elections supervised by the United Nations to insure that they are conducted fairly.

With respect to the statement made by the representative of the State of Viet-Nam, the United States reiterates its traditional position that peoples are entitled to determine their own future and that it will not join in an arrangement which would hinder this. Nothing in its declaration just made is intended to or does indicate any departure from this traditional position.

We share the hope that the agreements will permit Cambodia, Laos and Viet-Nam to play their part, in full independence and sovereignty, in the peaceful community of nations, and will enable the peoples of that area to determine their own future.

Ngo Dinh Diem offered his own, more emotionally charged view of the agreement.

Dear Compatriots,

You know the facts: a cease-fire concluded at Geneva without the concurrence of the Vietnamese delegation has surrendered to the Communists all the north and more than four provinces of the central part of our country.

The national Government, constituted less than two weeks

ago, in spite of its profound attachment to peace, has lodged the most solemn protest against that injustice. Our delegation at Geneva has not signed that agreement, for we cannot recognize the seizure by Soviet China—through its satellite the Viet Minh—of over half of our national territory. We can neither concur in the enslavement of millions of compatriots faithful to the nationalist ideal, nor to the complete destitution of those who, thanks to our efforts, will have succeeded in joining the zone left to us. Brutally placed before an accomplished fact, Vietnam cannot resort to violence, for that would be moving toward a catastrophe and destroying all hope of remaking one day a free Vietnam from the South to the North.

In spite of our grief, in spite of our indignation, let us keep our self-control and remain united in order to give our brother refugees help and comfort and begin at once the peaceful and difficult struggle which will eventually free our country from all foreign intervention, whatever it may be, and from all oppression.

We do not know Ho Chi Minh's private thoughts on the terms of the Geneva settlement, which gave his government considerably less than it had won on the battlefield, but we do know that he was deeply dismayed at pressure from his allies to sign the treaty. Publicly, at least, he put a positive spin on the agreement. In this pronouncement, titled "Long Live Peace, Unity, Independence, and Democracy in Vietnam," Ho expresses his hope that the promised election in two years' time would achieve the final victory he had been denied in Switzerland.

The Geneva Conference has ended. We have won a big victory in the diplomatic field. On behalf of the Government I cordially address myself to all compatriots, soldiers and political organizers.

1. For the sake of the peace, unity, independence and democracy of our homeland, our people, the army, cadres [political organizers] and the Government, closely united, enduring hardship and overcoming numerous difficulties, resolutely fought during the past eight, nine years and won brilliant victories. . . .

2. In order to achieve peace the first thing is the cessation of hostilities by the armed forces of both sides.

To ensure cessation of hostilities it is necessary to regroup the armed forces of the two sides in the two separate zones, that is, to readjust the areas occupied by the armed forces of each side.

Ho Chi Minh conducts an orchestra. Dressed in his customary informal garb, down to the sandals, Ho displays his many photogenic qualities.

Ho Chi Minh was known to the Vietnamese as "Bac Ho," or Uncle Ho. He was often photographed with little children, as in this 1951 picture that later became a popular poster.

The establishment of a military demarcation line is a temporary and transitional measure for carrying out the armistice, restoring peace and for making progress towards national unification by means of a general election. The demarcation line does not mean in any way a political or territorial boundary. . . .

3. We are fully determined honestly to adhere to the terms we have signed with the French Government and at the same time urge the French Government honestly to observe the terms it has signed with us.

We shall do our utmost to consolidate peace and shall be vigilant in relation to encroachments by the enemies of peace. We shall do everything for the holding of a free, general election throughout the country in order to achieve national unity.

I earnestly call on all who sincerely love their homeland, irrespective of social status, religious beliefs or political conviction, irrespective of the party they supported in the past, sincerely to cooperate with each other and work for the good of the nation and homeland, and to fight for the realization of peace, unity, independence and democracy in our beloved Viet Nam.

Given nation-wide unity, given the monolithic solidarity of the entire people we will, undoubtedly, win victory.

Long live peace, unity, independence and democracy in Viet Nam!

The Election of 1956

The promised elections of 1956 were not to be. Neither Ngo Dinh Diem nor his American sponsors wished to take the risk of having a communist government democratically elected, thereby giving it political legitimacy. President Dwight Eisenhower recalled the dilemma in his memoirs.

I am convinced that the French could not win the war because the internal political situation in Vietnam, weak and confused, badly weakened their military position. I have never talked or corresponded with a person knowledgeable in Indochinese affairs who did not agree that had elections been held as of the time of the fighting, possibly 80 per cent of the population would have voted for the Communist Ho Chi Minh as their leader.

Eisenhower's Vietnam

Convinced that the French would never understand Asian nationalism, Washington decided to take over the job of creating a modern, anti-Communist, independent nation-state in South Vietnam. By September 1954, the United States had begun to deal directly with President Diem in Saigon and five months later undertook the training and arming of the South Vietnamese Army (Army of the Republic of Vietnam).

In this letter to Ngo Dinh Diem, Eisenhower pledged his firm support in the expectation that, with United States help, Diem would be able to reform the government and win

the allegiance of the population.

Dear Mr. President:

I have been following with great interest the course of developments in Vietnam, particularly since the conclusion of the conference at Geneva. The implications of the agreement concerning Vietnam have caused grave concern regarding the future of a country temporarily divided by an artificial military grouping, weakened by a long and exhausting war, and faced with enemies without and by their subversive collaborators within.

Your recent requests for aid to assist in the formidable project of the movement of several hundred thousand loyal Vietnamese citizens away from areas which are passing under a de facto rule and political ideology which they abhor, are being fulfilled. I am glad that the United States is able to assist in this humanitarian effort. . . .

The purpose of this offer is to assist the Government of Vietnam in developing and maintaining a strong, viable state, capable of resisting attempted subversion or aggression through

President Dwight D. Eisenhower and Secretary of State John Foster Dulles greet Ngo Dinh Diem in Washington, D.C.

The truth is that the population of South Vietnam, like any other, is more responsive to fear and force than to an improved standard of living.

—General Samuel T. Williams in a memo to Ambassador Elbridge Durbrow, February 1960

military means. The Government of the United States expects that this aid will be met by performance on the part of the Government of Vietnam in undertaking needed reforms. It hopes that such aid, combined with your own continuing efforts, will contribute effectively toward an independent Vietnam endowed with a strong Government. Such a Government would, I hope, be so responsive to the nationalist aspirations of its people, so enlightened in purpose and effective in performance, that it will be respected both at home and abroad and discourage any who might wish to impose a foreign ideology on your free people.

Sincerely,
Dwight D. Eisenhower

The United States took upon itself the molding of a South Vietnamese government that was responsive to the people it governed if possible, but, more importantly, a government closely aligned with the United States and its ally in the Cold War. This was to be accomplished in many ways: international recognition of the South Vietnamese government, considerable U.S. aid funds, U.S. advisors for everything from military support to constitution writing, covert actions against the communists, and much more. So, despite its pledge to "take note of the [Geneva] agreements," the United States decided to ignore them and, indeed, to actively subvert their promise of unification of Vietnam through free elections and without foreign interference.

The Saigon Military Mission (SMM) was born in a Washington policy meeting early in 1954, when Dien Bien Phu was still holding out against the encircling Vietnamese. The SMM was to enter into Vietnam quietly and assist the anticommunist Vietnamese, rather than the French, in unconventional warfare. The French were to be kept as friendly allies in the process. The man in charge of the SMM was a former advertising executive turned CIA operative, Colonel Edward G. Lansdale.

The broad mission of his team was to undertake paramilitary operations against the Viet Minh and to wage political-psychological warfare such as the rumor campaign described in the following document. Later, after Geneva, the mission was modified to include sabotage operations in Communist areas rather than to wage unconventional warfare.

Highlights of the Year

A. EARLY DAYS

The Saigon Military Mission (SMM) started on 1 June 1954, when its Chief, Colonel Edward G. Lansdale, USAF, arrived in Saigon with a small box of files and clothes and a borrowed typewriter. . . .

The first rumor campaign was to be a carefully planted story of a Chinese Communist regiment in Tonkin taking reprisals against a Viet Minh village whose girls the Chinese had raped, recalling Chinese Nationalist troop behavior in 1945 and confirming Vietnamese fears of Chinese occupation under Viet Minh rule. The story was planted by soldiers of the Vietnamese Armed Psywar company in Hanoi dressed in civilian clothes. The troops received their instructions silently, dressed in civilian clothes, went on the mission, and failed to return. They had deserted to the Viet Minh. Weeks later, Tonkinese told an excited story of the misbehavior of the Chinese Divisions in Viet Minh territory. Investigated, it turned out to be the old rumor campaign, with

A U.S. Air Force C-47 distributes leaflets from the air. Psychological warfare was a major component of U.S. tactics both before and after the Geneva convention of 1953.

Vietnamese embellishments, leaving us to assume the deserting troops did their job regardless.

C. SEPTEMBER 1954

Earlier in the month [we] had engineered a black psywar strike in Hanoi: leaflets signed by the Viet Minh instructing Tonkinese on how to behave for the Viet Minh takeover of the Hanoi region in early October, including items about property, money reform, and a three-day holiday of workers upon takeover. The day following the distribution of these leaflets, refugee registration tripled. Two days later Viet Minh currency was worth half the value prior to the leaflets. The Viet Minh took to the radio to denounce the leaflets; the leaflets were so authentic in appearance that even most of the rank and file Viet Minh were sure that the radio denunciations were a French trick. . . .

D. OCTOBER 1954

Hanoi was evacuated on 9 October. The northern SMM team left with the last French troops, disturbed by what they had seen of the grim efficiency of the Viet Minh in their takeover, the contrast between the silent march of the victorious Viet Minh troops in their tennis shoes and the clanking armor of the well-equipped French whose western tactics and equipment had failed against the Communist military-political-economic campaign.

The northern team had spent the last days in Hanoi in contaminating the oil supply of the bus company for a gradual wreckage of engines in the buses, in taking the first actions for delayed sabotage of the railroad . . . and in writing detailed notes of potential targets for future paramilitary ops. The team had a bad moment when contaminating the oil. They had to work quickly at night, in an enclosed storage room. Fumes from the contaminant came close to knocking them out. Dizzy and weak-kneed, they masked their faces with handkerchiefs and completed the job. . . .

G. JANUARY 1955

The patriot we've named Trieu Dinh [a cover name] had been working on an almanac for popular sale. Noted Vietnamese astrologers were hired to write predictions about coming disasters to certain Viet Minh leaders and undertakings, and to predict unity in the south. Copies of the almanac were shipped by air to Haiphong and then smuggled into Viet Minh territory.

Dinh also had produced a Thomas Paine type series of essays on Vietnamese patriotism against the Communist Viet Minh.

These essays, circulated among influential groups in Vietnam, earned front-page editorials in the leading daily newspaper in Saigon. Circulation increased with the publication of these essays. The publisher is known to SMM as The Dragon Lady and is a fine Vietnamese girl, we had helped her keep her paper from being closed by the government, . . . and she found it profitable to heed our advice on the editorial content of her paper.

Arms and equipment for the Binh paramilitary team were being cached in the north in areas still free from the Viet Minh. . . .

We had smuggled into Vietnam about eight and a half tons of supplies for the Hao paramilitary group. They included fourteen agent radios, 300 carbines, 90,000 rounds of carbine ammunition, 50 pistols, 10,000 rounds of pistol ammunition, and 300 pounds of explosives.

J. APRIL 1955

Haiphong was taken over by the Viet Minh on 16 May. Our Binh and northern Hao teams were in place, completely equipped. It had taken a tremendous amount of hard work to beat the Geneva deadline, to locate, select, exfiltrate, train, infiltrate, equip the men of these two teams and have them in place, ready for actions required against the enemy. It would be a hard task to do openly, but this had to be kept secret from the Viet Minh, the International Commissions, . . . and even friendly Vietnamese.

Truong Nhu Tang, the son of a wealthy Saigon family, returned to Vietnam after studying in Paris. He joined the opposition to Diem, eventually becoming an official in the National Liberation Front, a nationalist coalition against Diem and the Americans led by the communists. . . . The following excerpts from his memoirs tell us a good deal about the choices faced by many educated Vietnamese at this time. In the first entry, Tang tells of his reaction to meeting Ho Chi Minh in 1945.

Looking on with a kind of confused interest, I was immediately struck by Ho Chi Minh's appearance. Unlike the others, who were dressed in Western-style clothes, Ho wore a frayed, high-collared Chinese jacket. On his feet he had rubber sandals. In contrast to the tense-looking younger men around him, he gave off an air of fragility, almost sickliness. But these impressions only contributed to the imperturbable dignity that enveloped him as though it

This leaflet, distributed by the South Vietnamese, encourages the defection of National Liberation Front (NLF) and North Vietnamese forces. The NLF and Hanoi stressed the power of human beings against high-tech warfare. This leaflet illustrates the contrary: the power of huge man-eating machines against puny individuals. The message reads: "Viet Cong Beware!!"

were something tangible. I had never thought of myself as a person especially sensitive to physical appearances, but Ho exuded a combination of inner strength and personal generosity that struck me with something like a physical blow. He looked directly at me, and at the others, with a magnetic expression of intensity and warmth.

Almost reflexively I found myself thinking of my grandfather. There was that same effortless communication of wisdom and caring with which my grandfather had personified for us the values of Confucian life. I was momentarily startled when Ho reached his arm out in a sweeping gesture, as if he were gathering us in. "Come, my children," he said and sat down on the steps. We settled around him, as if it were the most natural thing in the world. I sat next to him, already infusing this remarkable person, who seemed so like Grandfather, with the schoolboy reverence I had felt toward the personal heroes adopted from my reading of history: Gandhi, Sun Yat-sen, and especially Abraham Lincoln. Lost in thoughts like these, I was not observing my comrades closely, but my impression was that their attention too was riveted on Ho. He told us to call him Bac Ho—Uncle Ho—instead of Mr. President. Then he began asking each of us in turn about our families, our names, our studies, where we were from, how old we were. He wanted to know too about our feelings toward Vietnam's independence, a subject on which most of us had only the vaguest thoughts. We certainly hoped our country would be free. But beyond that we had little to contribute.

When Ho realized that among our group there were students from the North, South, and Center of the country, he said gently, but with great intensity, "Voilà! the youth of our great family of Vietnam. Our Vietnam is one, our nation is one. You must remember, though the rivers may run dry and the mountains erode, the nation will always be one." To Western ears such phrases may have sounded artificial. To ours the simple sentimentality was evocative. It was the language of slogan and poetry that Vietnamese leaders had always used to rally the people to a political cause. Ho went on to say that, when he was born, Vietnam was a nation of slaves. Since his own adolescence, he had been struggling for liberty, and that now we had the fortune to be free and independent citizens, a fortune that our parents and grandparents had not enjoyed. Eighty years of slavery had diminished the nation; now it was time to reestablish the heritage given to us by our ancestors and recover from our backwardness. If our people were to gain an honorable place among the peoples of the world, it would depend largely on us, on our efforts to study and learn and to contribute to the national family. It was a message that combined ardent and idealistic nationalism with a moving personal simplicity. Ho had created for us an atmosphere of family and country and had pointed to our own role in the great patriotic endeavor. Before an hour had passed, he had gained the heart of each one of us sitting around him.

Tang tells of a much different experience in this record of his subsequent life under Diem's government in the 1950s.

As a certified member of Saigon's small French-educated elite, I was sure I would not remain a passive observer forever . . . [some of my peers had joined the Diem administration. Others, like] another Paris graduate I ran into shortly afterward had gotten himself onto the wrong side of the administration. Au Truong Thanh, who was teaching law now at Saigon University, had participated in the Movement in Defense of Peace, formed the previous year to press for compliance with the Geneva-mandated unification elections. Made up primarily of intellectuals who had returned from France, together with some well-known Saigonese personalities, the group had been crushed by Diem and his chief American adviser, Colonel Edward Lansdale. Afraid that the movement might become an obstacle to his consolidation of power, Diem had accused the largely moderate or vaguely leftist members of being communists and had jailed some, expelled others, and sent a number into internal exile—including Nguyen Huu Tho, later to become the NLF's [National Liberation Front] first president.

But the petulant and unforgiving side of Diem's personality paled before the ruthless brutality with which he was treating the former anti-French guerrilla fighters. (I had known some of these men in Paris, and I was again beginning to talk to them.) Though Diem had established his own patriotism in years past, he had never been actively engaged in the French war and had spent the last four years of it outside Vietnam. As a result, he viewed the resistance veterans as rivals for power who had to be crushed. Labeling them all communist or procommunist, he was using the secret police and the blueshirted Republican Youth to hunt down these people—people who were considered by almost everyone else as freedom fighters.

It was a disastrous tactic. Fired by the compulsion to eliminate any potential opposition, Diem was irrevocably alienating himself from the emotional nationalism that had been the most potent

Perhaps naively and without consideration of the conflicting postwar interests of "big" nations themselves, the new government believed that by complying with the conditions of the wartime United Nations conferences it could invoke the benefits of those conferences in favor of its own independence.

—Arthur Hale, U.S. Information Agency, Memo to the State Department, Hanoi, October 1945

force in Vietnam for a decade. Instead of unfurling the banner of patriotism and rallying the country behind it, he had chosen to rely on his ability to cow or destroy everyone who might get in his way. In exercising power, he had resurrected the old feudal methods of closed government, complemented now by the advice and training provided by his American supporters. It was quickly becoming evident to me that Diem had an instinct for isolation and autocratic control and that he could only hope to make this approach to government work through brute force. In this endeavor the Americans would necessarily have to become full partners. . . . Diem's inability to conceive of himself as a popular leader meant that he would have to put his regime in permanent thrall to American aid and protection.

At least so it seemed to me. I was just then reaching my own decision not to cooperate with [Diem]. . . . The only question now was what form my opposition would take. As I mulled this problem over, the country officially became a republic—and Diem the first president. The 98.2 percent vote in favor was achieved through a variety of contrivances, including the use of voter-identification cards. These cards were stamped at the polls, and people with no stamp to show were likely to find themselves in trouble with the police later on. There was nothing special about Diem's cynical and blatant manipulation of the election. But it was both peculiar and disheartening to watch this unreconstructed mandarin utilizing the forms of democracy in order to placate his American protectors. . . . At that time a team from Michigan State University was in the country consulting with the government on the implementation of democratic political procedures. Whether these academic experts actually believed that the man who had just been elected president by a 98.2 percent vote could be reborn as a democrat, I don't know.

By December 1960 it was clear to the anti-Diem forces that a guerrilla war against Diem and his Americans backers was unavoidable. Southern opponents to Diem, communist and noncommunist alike, organized the National Liberation Front (NLF). Although a coalition of forces, the leadership nevertheless remained in the hands of the southern branch of the Workers (Communist) Party. However independent locally, the NLF at the same time accepted overall direction from Hanoi. Here are excerpts from the founding program of the NLF, issued in February 1961.

I. Overthrow the camouflaged colonial regime of the American imperialists and the dictatorial power of Ngo Dinh Diem, servant of the Americans, and institute a government of national democratic union. . . .

II. Institute a largely liberal and democratic regime. 1. Abolish the present constitution of the dictatorial powers of Ngo Dinh Diem, servant of the Americans. Elect a new National Assembly through universal suffrage. 2. Implement essential democratic liberties: freedom of opinion, of press, of assembly, of movement, of trade-unionism; freedom of religion without any discrimination; and the right of all patriotic organizations of whatever political tendency to carry on normal activities. 3. Proclaim a general amnesty for all political prisoners and the dissolution of concentration camps of all sorts; abolish . . . all . . . antidemocratic laws.

III. Establish an independent and sovereign economy, and improve the living conditions of the people. . . .

IV. Reduce land rent; implement agrarian reform with the aim of providing land to the tillers.

V. Develop a national and democratic culture and education. 1. Combat all forms of culture and education enslaved to Yankee fashions; develop a culture and education that is national, progressive, and at the service of the Fatherland and people. 2. Liquidate illiteracy. . . . 3. Promote science and technology and the national letters and arts. . . . 4. Watch over public health; develop sports and physical education.

VI. Create a national army devoted to the defense of the Fatherland and the people. . . .

VII. Guarantee equality between the various minorities and between the two sexes; protect the legitimate interests of foreign citizens established in Vietnam and of Vietnamese citizens residing abroad. . . .

VIII. Promote a foreign policy of peace and neutrality. 1. Cancel all unequal treaties that infringe upon the sovereignty of the

Using the side of a disabled U.S. military vehicle as a chalkboard, a National Liberation Front instructor teaches recruits how to operate an anti-tank grenade launcher.

In the early days of its struggle, the NLF relied on homemade equipment; here a column moves through the night using recycled perfume bottles as lanterns.

people and that were concluded with other countries by the servants of the Americans. 2. Establish diplomatic relations with all countries, regardless of their political regime. . . . 3. Develop close solidarity with peace-loving nations and neutral countries; develop free relations with the nations of Southeast Asia, in particular with Cambodia and Laos. 4. Stay out of any military bloc; refuse any military alliance with another country. 5. Accept economic aid from any country willing to help us without attaching any conditions to such help.

IX. Re-establish normal relations between the two zones, and prepare for the peaceful reunification of the country.

The peaceful reunification of the country constitutes the dearest desire of all our compatriots throughout the country. The National Liberation Front of South Vietnam advocates the peaceful reunification by stages on the basis of negotiations and through the seeking of ways and means in conformity with the interests of the Vietnamese nation. While awaiting this reunification, the governments of the two zones will, on the basis of negotiations, promise to banish all separatist and warmongering propaganda and not to use force to settle differences between the zones. Commercial and cultural exchanges between the two zones will be implemented; the inhabitants of the two zones will be free to move about throughout the country as their family and business interests indicate. The freedom of postal exchanges will be guaranteed.

X. Struggle against all aggressive war; actively defend universal peace.

Kennedy's War

On January 20, 1961, John F. Kennedy was sworn in as the 35th President of the United States. Kennedy embodied a spirit of America that espoused aggressive action—whether it was on the sports field or in the world. Kennedy believed that the United States had been chosen for a special mission to remake the world in its own image while making it secure for American economic and political interests. He spoke to that vision in his inaugural address. At that time the United States had fewer than 1,000 military personnel in Vietnam. They were technically listed as advisors and were primarily involved in the training and development of the Army of the Republic of Vietnam (ARVN). Over the course of the next two years, their number would rise to more than 16,000 and

**increasingly, though without publicity, they would engage
in combat missions.**

[The] same revolutionary beliefs for which our forebears fought
are still at issue around the globe—the belief that the rights of
man come not from the generosity of the state, but from the hand
of God.

We dare not forget today that we are the heirs of that first revolution.

Let the word go forth from this time and place, to friend and
foe alike, that the torch has been passed to a new generation of

*A page from the manuscript of John
F. Kennedy's inaugural address,
which announced a New Frontier.
Few Americans expected that the
New Frontier would turn out to be
located in Southeast Asia.*

Staff Sergeant Barry Sadler wrote a romantic ballad to his service, the Green Berets, which became an anthem for pro-war Americans. "The Ballad of the Green Berets" sold between 8 and 9 million albums and singles.

The Ballad of the Green Berets

The U.S. Army had originally created a Special Forces unit in 1952, and a small detachment was sent to Vietnam in 1957. The Special Forces were an elite corps of soldiers trained in traditional, psychological, and clandestine warfare; their goal was to counter guerrilla warfare around the world. President Kennedy took a particular interest in this elite corps, allowing them to wear a distinctive green beret and increasing their numbers from 2,500 to 10,000. Thousands of "Green Berets" were sent to Vietnam by the Kennedy administration to engage in counter-revolutionary activities. They became a popular symbol, epitomizing for some the "can do" ability of Americans to adjust to any situation, and for others an invading army dispatched to support dictatorial regimes aligned with Washington. One of their number, Sgt. Barry Sadler, immortalized them in a song.

Fighting soldiers from the sky,
fearless men who jump and die.
Men who mean just what they say,
the brave men of the Green Beret.

Chorus:
Silver wings upon their chest,
these are men, America's best.
One hundred men, we'll test today,
but only three, win the Green Beret.

Trained to live off Nature's land,
trained in combat - hand to hand.
Men who fight by night and day,
courage take, from the Green Beret.

Chorus

Back at home a young wife waits,
her Green Beret has met his fate.
He has died for those oppressed,
leaving her this last request.
"Put silver wings on my son's chest,
make him one of America's best.
He'll be a man they test one day.
Have him win, the Green Beret."

Americans—born in this century, tempered by war, disciplined by a hard and bitter peace, proud of our ancient heritage—and unwilling to witness or permit the slow undoing of those human rights to which this Nation has always been committed, and to which we are committed today at home and around the world.

Let every nation know, whether it wishes us well or ill, that we shall pay any price, bear any burden, meet any hardship, support any friend, oppose any foe, in order to assure the survival and the success of liberty.

This much we pledge—and more. . . .

To those new States whom we welcome to the ranks of the free, we pledge our word that one form of colonial control shall not have passed away merely to be replaced by a far more iron tyranny. We shall not always expect to find them supporting our view. But we shall always hope to find them strongly supporting their own freedom—and to remember that, in the past, those who foolishly sought power by riding the back of the tiger ended up inside. To those peoples in the huts and villages across the globe struggling to break the bonds of mass misery, we pledge our best efforts to help them help themselves, for whatever period is required—not because the Communists may be doing it, not because we seek their votes, but because it is right. If a free society cannot help the many who are poor, it cannot save the few who are rich.

During the spring and summer of 1963, as the war against the National Liberation Front went from bad to worse, the Diem government faced a new source of opposition, one of Diem's own making. Favoring fellow Catholics in a host of ways, Diem discriminated against those of the Buddhist faith. Angered at restrictions imposed on Buddhist public observances, leading monks led protest marches that were repressed with great force by Diem's brother, Ngo Dinh Nhu, who was head of the secret police. And then, one June morning, on a busy intersection in Saigon, the Venerable Thich Quang Duc, a Buddhist monk, assumed the lotus position and set himself on fire. The reporter Malcolm Browne, forewarned of the event, was present, and his pictures and descriptions had a powerful effect on American and international public opinion.

In his book *The New Face of War,* Browne described the death of Quang Duc and the protests that led up to it.

The whole thing had been touched off on Tuesday, May 8, 1963, when Buddhists observing the birthday of Buddha were forbidden to fly their flag in the streets. A pagoda protest by the powerful young monk Thich Tri Quang had been tape-recorded, and the Buddhists demanded permission to broadcast their recording on the local government radio station. Permission was denied, and several thousand Buddhist marchers led by monks headed from Hue's Tu Dam Pagoda for the radio station at the center of town.

As the marchers approached the radio station and surged around its entrance, the local military commander . . . had a bad case of the jitters. He ordered troops and armored cars to move in.

Several grenades, apparently thrown by trigger-happy soldiers, exploded in the midst of the crowd. A few of the marchers (including children) were crushed under the tracks of the armored vehicles. Eight persons were killed on the spot, and, of the scores wounded, several died later. . . .

"I'm not making a picture [*The Green Berets*] about Vietnam, I'm making a picture about good against bad. I happen to think that that's true about Vietnam, but even if it isn't as clear as all that, that's what you have to do to make a picture. It's all right, because we're in the business of selling tickets.

"It's the same thing as the Indians. Maybe we shouldn't have destroyed all those Indians, I don't know, but when you're making a picture, the Indians are the bad guys."

—*Mike Wayne, producer of* The Green Berets, *starring his father, John Wayne*

The Green Berets *was a novel by Robin Moore and a movie starring John Wayne. Artist Edward Sorel incorporated comments by the producer of the movie, Wayne's son Michael, in this caricature of Wayne, Ho Chi Minh, and the Hollywood Western movie version of the world. American soldiers often referred to the Vietnamese countryside as "Indian country."*

The Diem government, rather than back down, applied increasingly harsh measures against the Hue Buddhists, and the pleasant little city on the banks of the Perfume River became an armed camp. . . . [Demonstrations spread to Saigon and continued throughout May and early June. On the eleventh day, a car pulled up to Le Van Duyet Street.]

The monks in the car had gotten out, and one of them had opened its hood. From inside, he pulled a five-gallon gasoline can made of translucent plastic, filled to the brim with pink gasoline. . . . [One of the monks] placed a small brown cushion on the pavement, and the monk in the center sat down on it, crossing his legs in the traditional position of Buddhist meditation known as the "lotus position." This monk was the Venerable Thich Quang Duc, destined to be known throughout the world as the primary saint of modern Vietnamese Buddhism.

The three monks exchanged a few quiet words. The two who had flanked Quang Duc brought the gasoline container quickly to the center of the circle and poured most of it over the bowed head and shoulders of the seated monk. . . .

From about twenty feet away, I could see Quang Duc move his hands slightly in his lap striking a match. In a flash, he was sitting in the center of a column of flame, which engulfed his entire body. . . .

From time to time, a light breeze pulled the flames away from Quang Duc's face. His eyes were closed, but his features were twisted in apparent pain. He remained upright, his hands folded in his lap, for nearly ten minutes as the flesh burned from his head and body. . . .

Finally, Quang Duc fell backward, his blackened legs kicking convulsively for a minute or so. Then he was still, and the flames gradually subsided. . . .

Quang Duc's ashes were distributed to pagodas throughout the country. The yellow robes in which his body had been carried were cut into tiny swatches and distributed to Buddhist followers everywhere. . . . At one point, police tried to crack down on wearers of the yellow cloth, but there were too many of them. . . .

The Kennedy administration pressured Diem to reform, to settle with the Buddhists, to rid himself of Ngo Dinh Nhu. To no avail. Worse yet, rumors began to spread that Diem and Nhu had begun to make approaches to Hanoi for a settlement. Whether they were true or not, the possibility alarmed American officials, although some in Washington thought

In a terminal act of protest, the Buddhist monk Quang Duc publicly immolated himself in Saigon on June 11, 1963. The shocking image and what it indicated about popular dissatisfaction with the Diem government led to serious questions about the U.S. role in Vietnam.

this could be the occasion for an American withdrawal. Instead, the Kennedy administration decided to replace Diem and gave the green light for a coup by a junta of generals. Discussions with the generals, carried out by the new ambassador to Saigon, Henry Cabot Lodge, began in August and continued through the early fall of 1963. Washington expressed concern that the coup might not succeed, but Lodge insisted that any effort to discourage it would mean giving up on a change of government; in any event, the U.S. could not stop it by then. McGeorge Bundy, Kennedy's chief foreign policy advisor, disagreed about the power of the United States to forestall a coup but instructed Lodge to use his own judgment: if it looked as if it might fail, Lodge must try to stop it. However, once begun, it was crucial that it succeed.

On November 1, 1963, Diem was overthrown and both he and his brother were killed. It is important to note that the American public knew nothing about these events; they were kept secret. All that Americans were told was that Diem was a U.S. ally, with a deeply flawed government to be sure, who was overthrown by some of his own generals.

What follows are excerpts from the cable traffic between the Department of State in Washington, D.C., and the U.S. ambassador in Saigon, Henry Cabot Lodge, in the weeks and days prior to the coup.

Cablegram from Ambassador Lodge to Secretary of State Dean Rusk and Assistant Secretary of State Roger Hilsman, August 25, 1963:

Believe that chances of Diem's meeting our demands are virtually nil. . . . Therefore, propose we go straight to Generals with our demands, without informing Diem.

Cablegram from Lodge to Bundy, October 30, 1963:

My general view is that the U.S. is trying to bring this medieval country into the 20th century and that we have made considerable progress in military and economic ways but to gain victory we must also bring them into the 20th century politically and that can only be done by either a thoroughgoing change in the behavior of the present government or by another government. The Viet Cong problem is partly military but it is also partly psychological and political.

Cablegram from Bundy to Lodge, October 30, 1963:

a. U.S. authorities will reject appeals for direct intervention from either side. . . .

b. In the event of indecisive contest, U.S. authorities may in their discretion agree to perform any acts agreeable to both sides, such as removal of key personalities or relay of information. In such actions, however, U.S. authorities will strenuously avoid appearance of pressure on either side. It is not in the interest of

A birthday telegram from Ngo Dinh Diem to John F. Kennedy, May 1963. Relations between the two governments were frayed, but that did not prevent the combatants from observing the formalities.

The White House
Washington

1963 MAY 28   AM 6 29

WN1 67 VIA RCA

SAIGON 1200 MAY 27 1963

THE PRESIDENT

THE WHITE HOUSE WASHINGTONDC

SO 9210

ON THE OCCASION OF YOUR BIRTHDAY ANNIVERSARY I TAKE PLEASURE
IN EXTENDING TO YOUR EXCELLENCY MY WARMEST PERSONAL
CONGRATULATIONS TOGETHER WITH MY CORDIAL WISHES FOR YOUR
GOOD HEALTH AND HAPPINESS AS WELL AS FOR THE CONTINUED
PROSPERITY OF THE AMERICAN PEOPLE

NGO DINH DIEM PRESIDENT REPUBLIC VIETNAM

INCOMING TELEGRAM   *Department of State*   Fir
wkl

41

Action

SS

Info

EYES (.

Control: 7151
Rec'd: SEPTEMBER 11, 1963
3:16 A.M.

FROM: SAIGON

TO: Secretary of State

NO: 478, SEPTEMBER 11, 2 P.M. (SECTION I OF II)

IMMEDIATE

EYES ONLY FOR THE SECRETARY FROM LODGE

MY BEST ESTIMATE OF THE CURRENT SITUATION IN VIET NAM IS:

A. THAT IT IS WORSENING RAPIDLY;

B. THAT THE TIME HAS ARRIVED FOR THE US TO USE WHAT EFFECTIVE
SANCTIONS IT HAS TO BRING ABOUT THE FALL OF THE EXISTING GOVERN-
MENT AND THE INSTALLATION OF ANOTHER; AND
C. THAT INTENSIVE STUDY SHOULD BE GIVEN BY THE BEST BRAINS IN
THE GOVERNMENT TO ALL THE DETAILS, PROCEDURES AND VARIANTS
IN CONNECTION WITH THE SUSPENSION OF AID.

HEREWITH IS THE BACKGROUND FOR THIS PROPOSAL:

1. I DO NOT DOUBT THE MILITARY JUDGEMENT THAT THE WAR IN THE
COUNTRYSIDE IS GOING WELL NOW. BUT, AS ONE WHO HAS HAD LONG
CONNECTION WITH THE MILITARY, I DO DOUBT THE VALUE OF THE
ANSWERS WHICH ARE GIVEN BY YOUNG OFFICERS TO DIRECT QUESTIONS
BY GENERALS -- OR, FOR THAT MATTER, BY AMBASSADORS. THE URGE TO
GIVE AN OPTIMISTIC AND FAVORABLE ANSWER IS QUITE UNSURMOUNTABLE --
AND UNDERSTANDABLE. I, THEREFORE, DOUBT THE STATEMENT OFTEN
MADE THAT THE MILITARY ARE NOT AFFECTED BY DEVELOPMENTS IN
SAIGON AND THE CITIES GENERALLY.

2. THE FACT THAT SAIGON IS "ONLY ONE-SEVENTH" OF THE POPULATION

/DOES NOT

In the fall of 1963, Ambassador Henry Cabot Lodge cabled his estimate of the general situation in South Vietnam and starkly insisted that it was "worsening rapidly" despite optimistic reports by the military.

[the U.S. government] to be or appear to be either instrument of existing government or instrument of coup.

  c. In event of imminent or actual failure of coup, U.S. authorities may afford asylum in their discretion to those to whom there is any express or implied obligation of this sort. . . .

  d. But once a coup under responsible leadership has begun, and within these restrictions, it is in the interest of the U.S. Government that it should succeed.

Chapter 3

America's War

Three weeks after Diem's assassination, President John F. Kennedy was assassinated. On November 22, 1963, Lyndon Baines Johnson became the 36th President of the United States. Among his earliest acts was to send Secretary of Defense Robert McNamara to Saigon to assess the situation. Johnson had inherited Kennedy's war along with Kennedy's staff. Throughout the Kennedy administration he had been a strong supporter of the American effort; now, as commander in chief, he would have to assume full responsibility should the war escalate. The success of his own agenda, which included a new assault on economic and racial problems (the "War on Poverty"), would, he believed, hinge on his ability to resolve the war—one way or another. Despite private doubts about the war, Johnson's public stance and his actions made clear that he was not only going to continue to pursue Kennedy's policies, but would do so vigorously.

President Johnson's secretary of defense, Robert McNamara, upon returning from a two-day trip to Vietnam, gave Johnson little reason for optimism about winning the war. McNamara's assessment of the increasingly strained state of affairs in Vietnam is recorded in the following excerpted memorandum of December 21, 1963.

1. Summary. The situation is very disturbing. Current trends, unless reversed in the next 2–3 months, will lead to neutralization at best and more likely to a Communist-controlled state.

2. The new government is the greatest source of concern. It is indecisive and drifting. Although Minh [Duong Van "Big" Minh, head of the junta of military officers who led the coup against Diem] states that he, rather than the Committee of Generals, is making decisions, it is not clear that this is actually so. In any event, neither he nor the Committee are experienced in political administration and so far they

President Johnson, like many Americans, received tapes from relatives in Vietnam; here, in apparent exhaustion, he listens to one from his son-in-law, Captain Charles Robb.

show little talent for it. There is no clear concept on how to re-shape or conduct the strategic hamlet program; the Province Chiefs, most of whom are new and inexperienced, are receiving little or no direction; military operations, too, are not being effectively directed because the generals are so preoccupied with essentially political affairs. . . .

The Country Team [U.S. personnel in South Vietnam] is the second major weakness. It lacks leadership, has been poorly informed, and is not working to a common plan. A recent example of confusion has been conflicting USOM [United States Operations Mission] and military recommendations both to the Government of Vietnam and to Washington on the size of the military budget. Above all, [Ambassador] Lodge has virtually no official contact with [General] Harkins. Lodge sends in reports with major military implications without showing them to Harkins, and does not show Harkins important incoming traffic. . . .

Viet Cong progress has been great during the period since the coup, with my best guess being that the situation has in fact been deteriorating in the countryside since July to a far greater extent than we realized because of our undue dependence on distorted Vietnamese reporting. The Viet Cong now control very high proportions of the people in certain key provinces, particularly those directly south and west of Saigon. . . .In these key provinces, the Viet Cong have destroyed almost all major roads, and are collecting taxes at will. As remedial measures, we must get the government to re-allocate its military forces so that its effective strength in these provinces is essentially doubled. We also need to have major increases in both military and USOM staffs, to sizes that will give us a reliable, independent U.S. appraisal of the status of operations. Thirdly, realistic pacification plans must be prepared, allocating adequate time to secure the remaining government-controlled areas and work out from there. . . .

5. Infiltration of men and equipment from North Vietnam continues using (a) land corridors through Laos and Cambodia; (b) the Mekong River waterways from Cambodia; (c) some possible entry from the sea and the tip of the Delta. The best guess is that 1,000–1,500 Viet Cong cadres entered South Vietnam from Laos in the first nine months of 1963. The Mekong route (and also the possible sea entry) is apparently used for heavier weapons and ammunition and raw materials which have been turning up in increasing numbers in the south and of which we have captured a few shipments.

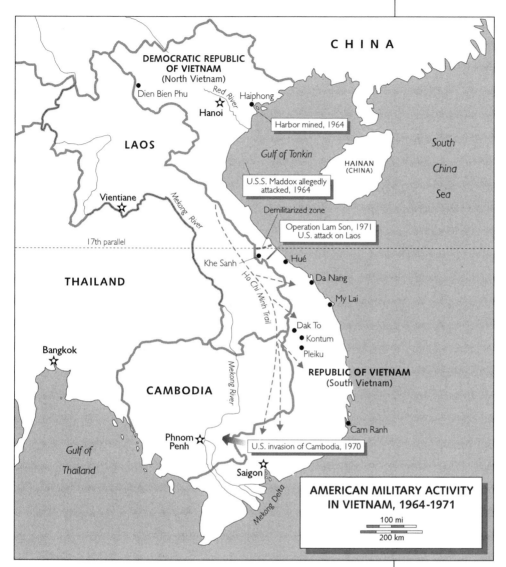

AMERICAN MILITARY ACTIVITY IN VIETNAM, 1964-1971

100 mi
200 km

To counter this infiltration, we reviewed in Saigon various plans providing for cross-border operations into Laos. On the scale proposed, I am quite clear that these would not be politically acceptable or even militarily effective. . . .

In general, the infiltration problem, while serious and annoying is a lower priority than the key problems discussed earlier. However, we should do what we can to reduce it.

There was never any consensus among policymakers and elected officials about how to proceeed in Vietnam. Democratic Senate majority leader Mike Mansfield, urged Johnson to seek a truce and subsequent neutralization of South Vietnam. McGeorge Bundy, on the other hand, argued for

moving ahead forcefully and decisively, conjuring up the ghost of the "domino theory" that President Eisenhower had first talked about.

To: The President
Date: January 6, 1964
From: McGeorge Bundy
Re: Senator Mansfield's Views on South Vietnam

1. To neutralize South Vietnam today, or even for the United States Government to seem to move in that direction, would mean the following:

a. A rapid collapse of anti-Communist forces in South Vietnam, and a unification of the whole country on Communist terms.

b. Neutrality in Thailand, and increased influence for Hanoi and Peking.

c. Collapse of the anti-Communist position in Laos.

d. Heavy pressure on Malaya and Malaysia.

e. A shift toward neutrality in Japan and the Philippines.

f. Blows to U.S. prestige in South Korea and Taiwan which would require compensating increases in American commitment there—or else further retreat.

2. We may have to move in these painful directions, but we should do so only when there is a much stronger demonstration that our present course cannot work. If we neutralize, it should not be because we have quit but because others have. Today a move in this direction would be regarded as betrayal by the new regime in Saigon and by all anti-Communist Vietnamese. There are enough of them to lose us an election.

3. The right course is to continue to strengthen our struggle against the Communist terror (which is exactly what it is). For this we need new and stronger leadership in the U.S. effort.

With all the conflicting reports and suggestions, and his own misgivings, President Johnson decided against making any momentous decisions on Vietnam until after the 1964 election, when he hoped to become President in his own right. Johnson, convinced that the United States could not pull out of Vietnam but aware of how unlikely current policy was to succeed, spent long hours on the phone with old political friends asking for their advice. Fortunately for future generations, he had all his phone calls recorded. This is an excerpt from a conversation with Senator Richard Russell

A North Vietnamese nurse dresses Air Force Captain Wilmer N. Grubb's wounds while a soldier guards him closely. The Air Force lost 2,257 aircraft over the period of the war; 2,584 air force personnel were killed in action.

(Democrat–Georgia), chairman of the powerful Senate Armed Services Committee, on June 11, 1964.

In the course of the conversation, Johnson refers to the Southeast Asia Treaty Organization (SEATO), created by the United States in 1954 as a regional defense organization. Signers included Australia, New Zealand, Pakistan, the Philippines, Thailand, France, Great Britain, and the United States. The alliance was intended to block communist expansion in Southeast Asia and signatories agreed that in the event of an armed attack against any of them or against any country considered vital to their security, there would be consultation for the "common defense." A separate agreement named Cambodia, southern Vietnam, and Laos as such vital areas. The obligation of the United States under the treaty was frequently used to justify the war in Vietnam.

LBJ: I'm confronted. I don't believe the American people ever want me to run [out on Vietnam]. If I lose it, I think that they'll say I've lost it. I've pulled in. At the same time, I don't want to commit us to a war. And I'm in a hell of a shape.

RUSSELL: We're just like a damn cow over a fence out there in Vietnam.

LBJ: . . . I've got a study being made now by the experts . . . whether Malaysia will necessarily go and India'll go and how much it'll hurt our prestige if we just got out and let some conference fail or something. . . . A fellow like A. W. Moursand [a businessman friend from Texas] said to me last night, "Goddamn, there's not anything that'll destroy you as quick as pulling out, pulling up stakes and running. American wants, by God, prestige and power." I said, "Yeah, but I don't want to kill these folks." He said, "I don't give a damn. I didn't want to kill 'em in Korea, but if you don't stand up for America, there's nothing that a fellow in Johnson City"—or Georgia or any other place—"they'll forgive you for anything except being weak." . . .

RUSSELL: . . . It'd take a half million men. They'd be bogged down in there for ten years. . . .

LBJ: Now Mansfield's got a four-page memo saying that I'm getting ourselves involved and I'm gonna get in another war if I do it anymore.

RUSSELL: . . . I, in a way, share some of his fears.

LBJ: I do too, but the fear the other way more.

RUSSELL: I don't know what the hell to do. I didn't ever want to get messed up down there. I do not agree with those brain trusters who say that this thing has got tremendous strategic and economic value and we'll lose everything in Southeast Asia if we lose Vietnam. . . . But as a practical matter, we're in there and I don't know how the hell you can tell the American people you're coming out. . . . They'll think that you've just been whipped, you've been ruined, you're scared. It'd be disastrous.

LBJ: I think that I've got to say that I didn't get in here, but we're in here by treaty [SEATO, Southeast Asia Treaty Organization] and our national honor's at stake. And if this treaty's no good, none of 'em are any good. Therefore we're there. And being there, we've got to conduct ourselves like men. That's number one. Number two, in our own revolution, we wanted freedom and we naturally look with sympathy with other people who want freedom and if you'll leave 'em alone and give 'em freedom, we'll get out tomorrow. . . . Third thing, we've got to try to find some proposal some way, like Eisenhower worked out in Korea.

RUSSELL: . . . I think the people, if you get some sort of agreement all the way around, would understand it. And I don't think that they're so damned opposed to the United Nations getting in there. And I don't think they'd be opposed to coming out. I don't think the American people want to stay in there. They've got enough sense to realize that it's just a matter of face, that we can't just walk off and leave those people down there.

The War Expands

Even as he expressed his doubts about the war, Johnson sought prior approval from Congress for any new military actions that might have to be undertaken. A congressional resolution on Vietnam had been under discussion in the cabinet for some time. Then, in the late summer of 1964, an incident in the Gulf of Tonkin proved an opportune occasion.

In response to what were said to have been two attacks by North Vietnam against American destroyers in international waters, Johnson ordered retaliatory bombing attacks on the North, and Congress gave the President broad warmaking powers on which Johnson quickly acted. In February 1965, bombing—already underway in the South and, although it was kept secret, in Laos—expanded to North Vietnam. It was code named Operation Rolling Thunder. In March 1965, Johnson ordered the first combat unit of U.S. marines to South Vietnam, and in July 1965 he made the decision to commit ground troops in force. The war was now, as many had predicted it would become, an American war.

The Gulf of Tonkin was a busy place. In addition to sabotage raids (called OPPLAN 34-A) conducted by South Vietnamese forces in which both the CIA and U.S. Special Forces participated, the U.S. Navy conducted intelligence-gathering missions in the Gulf. On August 2, 1964, North Vietnamese torpedo boats attacked the American destroyer U.S.S. *Maddox* and were readily repulsed. On August 4, the U.S.S. *Maddox* and another destroyer, the U.S.S. *Turner Joy,* reported a second attack, although their joint commander almost immediately expressed doubt as to whether it had actually occurred. Nevertheless, Johnson accused Hanoi of "open aggression on the high seas" and on this basis submitted a resolution to Congress authorizing him to take "all necessary measures to repel any armed attacks against the forces of the United States and to prevent further aggression." In addition, he asked for the authority to give military assistance to any member of SEATO. In a televised speech that same evening, he explained his actions to the American people.

My fellow Americans:

As President and Commander in Chief, it is my duty to the American people to report that renewed hostile actions against

President Johnson goes nose to nose with Senator Richard Russell, Democratic senator and good friend. Russell forcefully expressed his doubts about the policy on Vietnam to Johnson before the dispatch of American troops, but once they were committed, Russell supported government policy.

The U.S.S. Maddox, *in battle camouflage.*

United States ships on the high seas in the Gulf of Tonkin have today required me to order the military forces of the United States to take action in reply.

The initial attack on the destroyer U.S.S. *Maddox,* on August 2, was repeated today by a number of hostile vessels attacking two U.S. destroyers with torpedoes. The destroyers and supporting aircraft acted at once on the orders I gave after the initial act of aggression. We believe at least two of the attacking boats were sunk. There were no U.S. losses.

The performance of commanders and crews in this engagement is in the highest tradition of the United States Navy. But repeated acts of violence against the Armed Forces of the United States must be met not only with alert defense but with positive reply. That reply is being given as I speak to you tonight. Air action is now in execution against gunboats and certain supporting facilities in North Viet-Nam which have been used in these hostile operations.

In the larger sense this new act of aggression, aimed directly at our own forces, again brings home to all of us in the United States the importance of the struggle for peace and security in Southeast Asia. Aggression by terror against the peaceful villagers of South Viet-Nam has now been joined by open aggression on the high seas against the United States of America. The determination of all Americans to carry out our full commitment to the people and to the Government of South Viet-Nam will be redoubled by this outrage. Yet our response, for the present, will be limited and fitting. We Americans know, although others appear to forget, the risks of spreading conflict.

We still seek no wider war.

I have instructed the Secretary of State to make this position totally clear to friends and to adversaries and, indeed, to all. . . . Finally, I have today met with the leaders of both parties in the Congress of the United States, and I have informed them that I shall immediately request the Congress to pass a resolution making it clear that our Government is united in its determination to take all necessary measures in support of freedom and in defense of peace in Southeast Asia. I have been given encouraging assurance by these leaders of both parties that such a resolution will be promptly introduced, freely and expeditiously debated, and passed with overwhelming support.

It is a solemn responsibility to have to order even limited military action by forces whose overall strength is as vast and as awesome as those of the United States of America, but it is my considered conviction, shared throughout your Government, that firmness in the right is indispensable today for peace.

That firmness will always be measured. Its mission is peace.

Admiral James Stockdale, a U.S. Navy pilot (later a prisoner of war and a Vice-Presidential candidate in 1992), was on duty flying over the Gulf of Tonkin when the U.S. ships were allegedly attacked. Here he describes what he saw on August 4 as he flew over the U.S.S. *Maddox* and the U.S.S. *Turner Joy* and his reaction upon hearing of American "reprisal" bombings against the Vietnamese.

Night of Tuesday, August 4, 1964

I maneuvered close to the water, unencumbered by a wing man, lights off, trying to find whatever boat the destroyers were talking about and blast it immediately. I had the best seat in the house from which to detect boats—if there were any. . . . Time and again I flew right over the *Maddox* and the *Joy,* throttled back, lights out, like a near-silent stalking owl. . . .

When the destroyers were convinced they had some battle action going, I zigged and zagged and fired where they fired unless it looked like I might get caught in their shot patterns or

Hard Questions

The American media generally reported what administration officials told them to report. In this unusual case, an NBC-TV journalist, Elie Abe, questions Secretary of State Dean Rusk about why the Vietnamese would launch an allegedly unprovoked attack.

Question (Elie Abel): What explanation, then, can you come up with for this unprovoked attack?

Answer (Dean Rusk): Well I haven't been able, quite frankly, to come to a fully satisfactory explanation. There is a great gulf of understanding between that world and our world, ideological in character. They see what we think of as the real world in wholly different terms. Their very processes of logic are different. So that it's very difficult to enter into each other's minds across that great ideological gulf. I can't come to a rational explanation of it. Perhaps they will offer one some day. But thus far we have to take it as we see it. And the essential fact was that our vessels were being attacked on the high seas by these boats and we had to do something about it. . . .

The Real Story

Publicly, administration officials were unwilling to admit that the U.S. Navy destroyers may have been engaged in provocative military action against action North Vietnam. But privately they knew better. This excerpt is from President Johnson's conversation with Robert Anderson, President Eisenhower's former Secretary of the Treasury, took place on August 3, 1964, the day after the U.S.S. Maddox was engaged in a brief firefight in the Gulf of Tonkin and a day before the White House began a public campaign arguing that the attack was "unprovoked."

LBJ: There have been some covert operations in that area that we have been carrying on—blowing up some bridges and things of that kind, roads and so forth. So I imagine they wanted to put a stop to it. So they . . . fired and we respond immediately with five-inch [artillery shells] from the destroyer and with planes overhead. And we . . . knock one of 'em out and cripple the other two. Then we go right back where we were with that destroyer and with another one, plus plenty of planes standing by. . . .

ANDERSON: . . . You're going to be running against a man who's a wild man on this subject [Barry Goldwater, the Republican candidate for President]. Any lack of firmness he'll make up.

LBJ: What happened was we've been playing around up there and they came out, gave us a warning, and we knocked hell out of 'em.

ANDERSON: That's the best thing in the world you could have done—just knock hell out of 'em.

LBJ: And we've got our people right there and we haven't pulled out. We've pulled up.

unless they had told me to fire somewhere else . . . no wakes or dark shapes other than those of the destroyers were ever visible to me. . . .

. . .[After landing I] wheel[ed] into the ready room I had hurriedly left three hours before, I came face-to-face with about ten assorted ship's company, air group, and staff intelligence officers—all with sheepish grins on their faces. "What in hell has been going on out there?" they laughingly asked. . . ."Did you see any boats?"

"Not a one. No boats, no boat wakes, no ricochets off boats, no boat gunfire, no torpedo wakes—nothing but black sea and American firepower. But for goodness' sake, I must be going crazy.

I was handed a few sheets of a rough communication log—on which were transcribed all the messages from the *Maddox* since I had left the ship . . . about sonars not operating properly, about radars not locking on targets, about probable false targets, about false perceptions due to lack of visibility. But still, it mainly reflected the tone of victimized vessels being attacked—that is, until I got to the last page and a half; then, as I read down them, everything seemed to flip around. There was denial of the correctness of immediately preceding messages, doubt about the validity of whole blocks of messages, ever more skeptical appraisal of detection equipment's performance, the mention of overeager sonar operators, the lack of any visual sightings of boats by the destroyers, and finally there were lines expressing doubt that there had been any boats out there that night at all. The commodore urged a complete evaluation of the mixup before any further action be taken.

Wednesday, August 5, 1964

After what seemed like a very short night, I felt myself being shaken. . . . "Who are you?" I asked.

"I'm the junior officer of the deck, sir. The captain sent me down to wake you. We just got a message from Washington telling you to prepare to launch strikes against the beach, sir. . . . The captain wants you to start getting ready to lead the big one, sir. Please get up, sir; your target is Washington's priority number one [against oil-storage facilities in the city of Vinh]."

"What's the idea of the strikes?"

"Reprisal, sir."

"Reprisal for what?"

"For last night's attack on the destroyers, sir."

I flipped on my bed lamp and the young officer left. I felt like

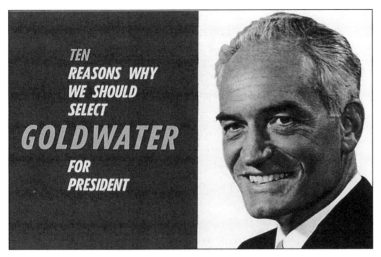

Conservative Arizona senator Barry Goldwater ran for President against Lyndon B. Johnson in 1964. His support for increased military action in Vietnam included the call to carry the war to North Vietnam, which Johnson was soon to do.

I had been doused with ice water. How do I get in touch with the president? He's going off half-cocked.

We were about to launch a war under false pretenses, in the face of the on-scene military commander's advice to the contrary. . . .

I felt it was a bad portent that we seemed to be under the control of a mindless Washington bureaucracy, vain enough to pick their own legitimacies regardless of evidence.

There was considerable skepticism in Congress about how the United States was conducting the war in Vietnam. Nevertheless, when it came to vote on a resolution that would give the President a free hand to escalate the war, 88 senators, spurred on by the idea of retaliation against what they believed to be repeated and unprovoked attacks on U.S. ships, voted in favor of the Tonkin Gulf Resolution. Only two senators refused to give the President the benefit of the doubt: Wayne Morse (Democrat–Oregon) and Ernest Gruening (Democrat–Alaska).

President Johnson relied on J. William Fulbright, chairman of the Senate Committee on Foreign Relations, to steer the resolution through the Senate. During the August 6, 1964 debate in the Senate, Gaylord Nelson, a liberal Democrat from Wisconsin, raised hard questions, which Fulbright fended off.

MR. NELSON [Gaylord Nelson, Democrat–Wisconsin] . . . Am I to understand that it is the sense of Congress that we are saying to the executive branch: "If it becomes necessary to prevent further aggression, we agree now, in advance, that you may land

A Hard-liner

One of the major issues in the 1964 Presidential campaign was the escalating war in Vietnam. Senator Barry Goldwater of Arizona, the Republican candidate for President, urged a stronger line on Vietnam.

Was it strength that was responsible for the attacks on our destroyers in the Gulf of Tonkin? Or was it the enemy's doubt of our strength and doubt of our will to use it?

And I charge that our policies have become so involved, so twisted with diplomatic red tape that the enemy might well have wondered if we would accept their attacks at sea on the same basis that we have been accepting their attacks on land.

And I support, before anyone gets the wrong idea, as does my party, as do all Americans, the President's firm action in response. But I must point out that it was just that, a response—an incident not a program or a new policy; a tactical reaction, not a new winning strategy.

Yes, all of us support the President in this strong, right action. No, we will not let this one action obscure a multitude of other needed actions.

And no, we will not let our support today silence our basic criticism that the war in Vietnam—and let's call it what it is, a war—that the war in Vietnam is being fought under policies that obscure our purposes, confuse our allies, particularly the Vietnamese, and encourage the enemy to prolong the fighting.

We must, instead, prosecute the war in Vietnam with the object of ending it along with the threats to peace that it poses all over the world.

A Critic Speaks

Senator Wayne Morse was the Senate's most outspoken critic of Johnson's policies toward Vietnam and he rarely passed up the opportunity to publicly comment on it.

It is my position that the United States was a constructive aggressor from the very beginning of the attacks on North Vietnam. Our country supplied the South Vietnamese patrol boats. Our country equipped them. Our country trained the personnel. Officials of our Government, both military and civilian, were fully aware at all times of the aggression of the South Vietnamese against the North Vietnamese islands and shore targets. Our government helped prepare and direct the plans.

Therefore, for the Secretary of Defense, military naval commanders, and the White House to allege that our destroyers were conducting a routine patrol on Tonkin Bay at the time of the North Vietnamese attack on the *Maddox* is simply not in accordance with the facts.

as many divisions as deemed necessary, and engage in a direct military assault on North Vietnam if it becomes the judgment of the Executive, the Commander in Chief, that this is the only way to prevent further aggression[?]"

MR. FULBRIGHT [J. William Fulbright, Democrat–Arkansas] . . . I do not know what the limits are. I do not think this resolution can be determinative of that fact. I think it would indicate that he [the President] would take reasonable means first to prevent any further aggression, or repel further aggression against our own forces, and that he will live up to our obligations under the SEATO treaty and with regard to the protocol states. I do not know how to answer the Senator's question and give him an absolute assurance that large numbers of troops would not be put ashore. I would deplore it. And I hope the conditions do not justify it now. . . .

On August 7, 1964, Congress passed the Tonkin Gulf Resolution, allowing Johnson to increase involvement in Vietnam.

Whereas naval units of the Communist regime in Vietnam, in violation of the principles of the Charter of the United Nations and of international law, have deliberately and repeatedly attacked United States naval vessels lawfully present in international waters, and have thereby created a serious threat to international peace; and

Whereas these attacks are part of a deliberate and systematic campaign of aggression that the Communist regime in North Vietnam has been waging against its neighbors and the nations joined with them in the collective defense of their freedom; and

Whereas the United States is assisting the peoples of southeast Asia to protect their freedom and has no territorial, military or political ambitions in that area, but desires only that these peoples should be left in peace to work out their own destinies in their own way: Now, therefore, be it *Resolved by the Senate and House of Representatives of the United States of America in Congress assembled,*

That the Congress approves and supports the determination of the President, as commander in chief, to take all necessary measures to repel any armed attack against the forces of the United States and to prevent further aggression.

Bombing of the North, begun as an immediate response to the alleged second attack in the Gulf of Tonkin, was transformed, by February 1965, into a new policy of "sustained

reprisal." McGeorge Bundy explained why in a memorandum drafted early in the month.

We believe that the best available way of increasing our chance of success in Vietnam is the development and execution of a policy of sustained reprisal against North Vietnam—a policy in which air and naval action against the North is justified by and related to the whole Viet Cong campaign of violence and terror in the South.

While we believe that the risks of such a policy are acceptable, we emphasize that its costs are real. It implies significant U.S. air losses even if no full air war is joined, and it seems likely that it would eventually require an extensive and costly effort against the whole air defense system of North Vietnam. U.S. casualties would be higher—and more visible to American feelings—than those sustained in the struggle in South Vietnam.

Yet measured against the costs of defeat in Vietnam, this program seems cheap. And even if it fails to turn the tide—as it may—the value of the effort seems to us to exceed the cost.

Bundy outlined the plan in more detail.

1. In partnership with the Government of Vietnam, we should develop and exercise the option to retaliate against any VC act of violence to persons or property.

2. In practice, we may wish at the outset to relate our reprisals to those acts of relatively high visibility. . . . Later, we might retaliate against the assassination of a province chief, but not necessarily the murder of a hamlet official; we might retaliate against a bomb thrown in a crowded café, but not necessarily to a shot fired into a small shop in Saigon.

3. Once a program of reprisals is clearly underway, it should not be necessary to connect each specific act against North Vietnam to a particular outrage in the South. It should be possible, for example, to publish weekly lists of outrages in the South and to have it clearly understood that these outrages are the cause of such action against the North as may be occurring in the current period. . . . We must keep it clear at every stage both to Hanoi and to the world, that our reprisals will be reduced or stopped when outrages in the South are reduced or stopped-and that we are not attempting to destroy or conquer North Vietnam. . . .

We cannot assert that a policy of sustained reprisal will succeed in changing the course of the contest in Vietnam. It may fail,

FOREIGN LANGUAGES PUBLISHING HOUSE
HANOI — 1965

The North Vietnamese were confident that the Americans, like the French, would be defeated. They expressed this view in many forms, including cartoons. The cover of this collection shows determined, if clumsy, American troops goose stepping like Nazis toward South Vietnam only to exit as shadowy, wounded figures.

and we cannot estimate the odds of success with any accuracy—they may be somewhere between 25% and 75%. What we can say is that even if it fails, the policy will be worth it. At minimum it will damp down the charge that we did not do all we could have done, and this charge will be important in many countries, including our own. Beyond that, a reprisal policy—to the extent that it demonstrates U.S. willingness to employ this new norm in counter-insurgency—will set a higher price for the future upon all adventures of guerrilla warfare, and it should therefore somewhat increase our ability to deter such adventures. We must recognize, however, that ability will be gravely weakened if there is failure for any reason in Vietnam.

The Public Debate

By June 1965, there were 82,000 combat troops in South Vietnam and General Westmoreland was asking for more: 175,000 by the end of the year and another 100,000 in 1966. Alarmed, some of President Johnson's advisers raised fundamental questions about the entire effort. Among them was George Ball, undersecretary of state, who had already expressed his opposition to Vietnam policy in a 67-page single-spaced memorandum addressed to Dean Rusk, McGeorge Bundy, and Robert McNamara in early October 1964. He did so again in a second memorandum in early July 1965.

For a week in late July, President Johnson held a series of high-level meetings, in part to discuss the request, but more importantly, to build consensus around the decisions he had already reached. Once more Ball dissented, and he was joined by Presidental advisor Clark Clifford, Vice President Hubert H. Humphrey, and several staff members in the White House and the State Department. But these men were a "loyal opposition," and none made their dissent public.

George Ball's memoranda are among the most extensive explorations of why full-scale U.S. entry into the war was unwise. The June 29, 1965, memorandum below, addressed to Dean Rusk, Robert McNamara, McGeorge Bundy, William Bundy, Jim McNaughton, and Leonard Unger, is an example. The situation he describes was well known to officials in Washington, if not to the people of the United States. Ball's arguments did not prevail, but his predictions proved largely accurate.

In the safety of the huge naval base at Cam Ranh Bay, General Westmoreland seems to be whispering words of confidence and certainty in President Johnson's ear.

It should by now be apparent that we have to a large extent created our own predicament. In our determination to rally support, we have tended to give the South Vietnamese struggle an exaggerated and symbolic significance (Mea culpa, since I personally participated in this effort).

The problem for us now—if we determine not to broaden and deepen our commitments—is to re-educate the American people and our friends and allies that:

a. The phasing out of American power in South Vietnam should not be regarded as a major defeat—either military or political—but a tactical redeployment to more favorable terrain in the overall cold war struggle;

b. The loss of South Vietnam does not mean the loss of all of Southeast Asia to the Communist power. . . .

d. The Viet Cong—while supported and guided from the North—is largely an indigenous movement. Although we have emphasized its cold war aspects, the conflict in South Vietnam is essentially a civil war within that country.

e. Our commitment to the South Vietnamese people is of a wholly different order from our major commitments elsewhere—to Berlin, to NATO, to South Korea, etc. . . .

A Compromise Solution in South Vietnam

1. *A Losing War:* The South Vietnamese are losing the war to the Viet Cong. No one can assure you that we can beat the Viet Cong or even force them to the conference table on our terms, no matter how many hundred thousand white, foreign (U.S.) troops we deploy.

No one has demonstrated that a white ground force of whatever size can win a guerrilla war—which is at the same time a civil war between Asians—in jungle terrain in the midst of a population that refuses cooperation to the white forces (and the South Vietnamese) and thus provides a great intelligence advantage to the other side. . . .

2. *The Question to Decide:* Should we limit our liabilities in South Vietnam and try to find a way out with minimal long-term costs?

The alternative—no matter what we may wish it to be—is almost certainly a protracted war involving an open-ended commitment of U.S. forces, mounting U.S. casualties, no assurance of a satisfactory solution, and a serious danger of escalation at the end of the road.

Half Truths

U.S. officials were optimistic in public, insisting the war was winnable and necessary to defend freedom in Vietnam. However, they were more honest about their motives in private, as in this paper prepared by John McNaughton, assistant secretary of defense for international security affairs, on March 10, 1965.

US aims:

70% — To avoid a humiliating US defeat (to our reputation as a guarantor).

20% — To keep SVN (and then adjacent) territory from Chinese hands.

10% — To permit the people of SVN to enjoy a better, freer way of life.

Also — To emerge from crisis without unacceptable taint from methods used.

Not — To "help a friend," although it would be hard to stay if asked out.

3. *Need for a Decision Now:* So long as our forces are restricted to advising and assisting the South Vietnamese, the struggle will remain a civil war between Asian peoples. Once we deploy substantial numbers of troops in combat it will become a war between the U.S. and a large part of the population of South Vietnam, organized and directed from North Vietnam and backed by the resources of Moscow and Peiping [Beijing].

The decision you face now, therefore, is crucial. Once large numbers of U.S. troops are committed to direct combat, they will begin to take heavy casualties in a war they are ill-equipped to fight in a non-cooperative if not downright hostile countryside.

Once we suffer large casualties, we will have started a well-nigh irreversible process. Our involvement will be so great that we cannot—without national humiliation—stop short of achieving our objectives. Of the two possibilities I think humiliation would be more likely than the achievement of our objectives—even after we have paid terrible costs.

4. *Compromise Solution:* Should we commit U.S. manpower and prestige to a terrain so unfavorable as to give a very large advantage to the enemy—or should we seek a compromise settlement which achieves less than our stated objectives and thus cut our losses while we still have the freedom of maneuver to do so.

5. *Costs of a Compromise Solution:* The answer involves a judgment as to the cost to the U.S. of such a compromise settlement in terms of our relations with the countries in the area of South Vietnam, the credibility of our commitments, and our prestige around the world. In my judgment, if we act before we commit a substantial U.S. truce [sic] to combat in South Vietnam we can, by accepting some short-term costs, avoid what may well be a long-term catastrophe. I believe we tended grossly to exaggerate the costs involved in a compromise solution.

Writing to the President on July 20, 1965, Secretary of Defense Robert McNamara, a strong supporter of an increased military commitment, outlined three alternative policies that were, on the surface, equally plausible. But he described them in such a way that only one, escalation, made any sense.

Options open to us:

a. Cut our losses and withdraw under the best conditions that can be arranged—almost certainly conditions humiliating the U.S.

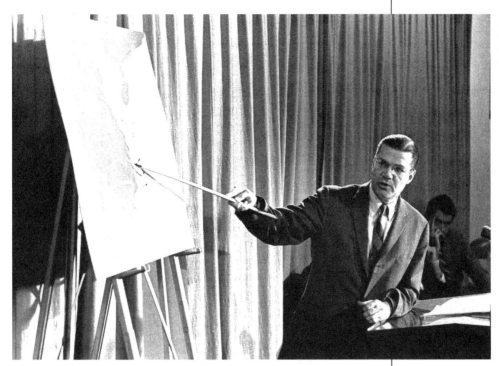

Equipped with a map, a pointer, and severely disciplined hair, Secretary of Defense Robert S. McNamara frequently briefed reporters, assuring them and, through them, the country, that all was well in South Vietnam.

and very damaging to our future effectiveness on the world scene.

b. Continue at about the present level, with the US forces limited to say, 75,000, holding on and playing for the breaks—a course of action which, because our position would grow weaker, almost certainly would confront us later with a choice between withdrawal and an emergency expansion of forces, perhaps too late to do any good.

c. Expand promptly and substantially the US military pressure against the VC in the South and maintain the military pressure against the NVNese in the North while launching a vigorous efforts on the political side to lay the groundwork for a favorable outcome by clarifying our objectives and establishing channels of communication. . . . This alternative would stave off defeat in the short run and offer a good chance of producing a favorable settlement in the longer run; at the same time, it would imply a commitment to see a fighting war clear through a considerable cost in casualties and materiel and would make any later decision to withdraw even more difficult and even more costly than would be the case today.

My recommendations . . . below are based on the choice of the third alternative as the course of action involving the best odds of the best outcome with the most acceptable cost to the US. . . . Increase by October . . . up to approx. 175,000. . . . It should be understood that the deployment of more men (perhaps

Sergeant P. L. Thompson poses on the throne of the emperor Tu Duc on February 24, 1968. American military control of the city was absolute and the photograph makes a political claim as well.

100,000) may be necessary in early 1966, and that the deployment of additional forces therefore is possible but will depend on developments.

Ask Congress to authorize call up of 235,000 men in Reserve and National Guard; increase regular forces by 375,000 men. By mid-66 US would have 600,000 additional men as protection against contingencies.

The growing severity of the debate over Vietnam—both inside the administration and in the streets—created a political problem for President Johnson, so he decided to talk directly to the people in a televised speech on July 28, 1965.

Why must young Americans, born into a land exultant with hope and with golden promise, toil and suffer and sometimes die in such a remote and distant place?

The answer, like the war itself, is not an easy one, but it echoes clearly from the painful lessons of half a century. Three times in my lifetime, in two World Wars and in Korea, Americans have gone to far lands to fight for freedom. We have learned at a terrible and a brutal cost that retreat does not bring safety and weakness does not bring peace.

It is this lesson that has brought us to Viet-Nam. This is a different kind of war. There are no marching armies or solemn declarations. Some citizens of South Viet-Nam at times, with understandable grievances, have joined in the attack on their own government.

But we must not let this mask the central fact that this is really war. It is guided by North Viet-Nam and it is spurred by Communist China. Its goal is to conquer the South, to defeat American power, and to extend the Asiatic dominion of communism.

There are great stakes in the balance. Most of the non-Communist nations of Asia cannot, by themselves and alone, resist the growing might and the grasping ambition of Asian communism. Our power, therefore, is a very vital shield. If we are driven from the field in Viet-Nam, then no nation can ever again have the same confidence in American promise, or in American protection.

In each land the forces of independence would be considerably weakened, and an Asia so threatened by Communist domination would certainly imperil the security of the United States itself.

We did not choose to be the guardians at the gate, but there is no one else.

Nor would surrender in Viet-Nam bring peace, because we learned from Hitler at Munich that success only feeds the appetite of aggression.

This then, my fellow Americans, is why we are in Viet-Nam.

The intensity of the war quickened. By 1966, substantial areas of South Vietnam had become "free-fire zones," populated areas from which, it was presumed, all "innocent" civilians had been evacuated and only the enemy remained. Anything and anybody left were fair game. Such zones were

The Numbers of War

The nature of the war in these years can be captured by statistics. Although South Vietnam was a friendly country, U.S. forces had dropped 1,388,000 tons of bombs on it by 1969. Ground ammunition expended amounted to 1,374,000 tons during the same period; and in the first nine months of 1967, varieties of highly toxic crop defoliants (most of it Agent Orange) were sprayed on 965,006 acres of land. Overall, American troops expended 500 times the quantity of ammunition used by the NLF; and if the bombing of the north is added to the tonnage dropped on the south, the total is a stunning 4.5 million tons (1965–1969) or 500 pounds of explosives for every Vietnamese man, woman, and child. And still General Westmoreland called for more American troops, requesting an additional 200,000 in 1968.

Say NO to this Johnson's war !
Let the Vietnamese people themselves
settle their own affairs !
Go home NOW — ALIVE !

Merry Christmas

Both sides encouraged defection or desertion. The NLF secretly distributed this nostalgic Christmas card to presumably homesick American soldiers, encouraging them to say no to the war.

Losing Mr. Average Citizen

David Halberstam, who had covered the war from the earliest days for the New York Times, *assessed the importance of CBS anchorman Walter Cronkite's turn against the war.*

Most of the press accepted President Johnson's explanations of U.S. policy, and those who were critical addressed its implementation rather than its substance. In this context, Cronkite's support for a negotiated end to the war hurt Johnson deeply.

Cronkite's reporting did change the balance; it was the first time in American history a war had been declared over by an anchorman. In Washington, Lyndon Johnson watched and told his press secretary, George Christian, that it was a turning point, that if he had lost Walter Cronkite he had lost Mr. Average Citizen. It solidified his decision not to run again. . . . In his own mind Walter had tried to remain straight and tried to report the war as it was. So when Cronkite gave his post-Tet report . . . Johnson . . . realized that he had lost the center . . . and thus his own consensus was in serious jeopardy. . . . He found himself believing that if Walter Cronkite was reporting these things, he must know something.

enlarged to areas of several square miles within which saturation bombing by B-52 aircraft or shelling by massed artillery cleared the land and made it uninhabitable by either National Liberation Front troops or the local peasantry. It was this decimation of the land, more than anything else, that caused people to flee to refugee camps in the safe areas near Saigon and other cities.

After the January 1968 Tet offensive, in which, to the apparent surprise of General Westmoreland, combined NLF and North Vietnamese troops attacked no fewer than 34 provincial centers, 64 district towns, and every major city in the south, President Johnson rejected requests for any increase in the number of U.S. troops. On March 31, Johnson called a bombing halt in much of the north (bombing of the south continued) and declared he would devote the remainder of his Presidential term to seeking peace rather than reelection. Although the Tet offensive was, technically, a military defeat for the NLF, politically it must be counted as a victory. Perhaps the single most influential establishment figure to turn against the war in its aftermath was the revered CBS-TV anchorman Walter Cronkite. On February 27, 1968, CBS broadcast a special half-hour program in which Cronkite reported on his recent trip to Vietnam.

Tonight, back in more familiar surroundings, we'd like to sum up our findings in Vietnam, an analysis that must be speculative, personal, subjective. Who won and who lost in the great Tet offensive against the cities? I'm not sure. The Viet Cong did not win by a knockout, but neither did we. The referees of history may make it a draw. . . .

The South Vietnamese goverment produced "safe conduct passes" for North Vietnamese who might wish to surrender. Such passess promised the bearer "a warm welcome, a guarantee of safety, and proper treatment."

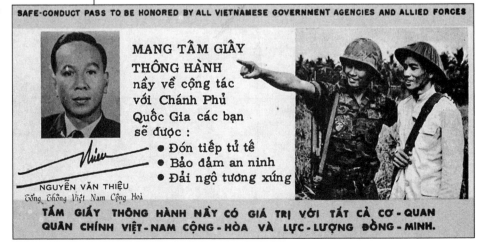

We have been too often disappointed by the optimism of the American leaders, both in Vietnam and Washington, to have faith any longer in the silver linings they find in the darkest clouds. They may be right, that Hanoi's winter-spring offensive has been forced by the Communist realization that they could not win the longer war of attrition, and that the Communists hope that any success in the offensive will improve their position for eventual negotiations. It would improve their position, and it would also require our realization, that we should have had all along, that any negotiations must be just that—negotiations, not the dictation of peace terms. . . .

To say that we are closer to victory today is to believe, in the face of the evidence, the optimists who have been wrong in the past. To suggest that we are on the edge of defeat is to yield to unreasonable pessimism. To say that we are mired in stalemate seems the only realistic, yet unsatisfactory, conclusion. On the off chance that military and political analysts are right, in the next few months we must test the enemy's intentions, in case this is indeed his last big gasp before negotiations. But it is increasingly clear to this reporter that the only rational way out then will be to negotiate, not as victors, but as an honorable people who lived up to their pledge to defend democracy, and did the best they could.

Refugees evacuate My Tho, the capital of Dinh Tuong province, during the Tet offensive. Between 1964 and 1969, 4 million South Vietnamese were displaced; by 1975, the figure had risen to 12 million out of a total South Vietnamese population of 24 million. The war reached the cities directly during the Tet offensive when 27 of South Vietnam's 44 provincial capitals, 5 of 6 autonomous cities, and 64 of 245 district towns were attacked. More than 14,300 civilians died during the offensive, in cross fire, from U.S. bombing, and, in Hue, from the deliberate targeting of Saigon government officials. 800,000 became refugees.

Selling Patriotism

In the conflict between Vietnam and the United States, both sides appealed to the patriotism of their people in the effort to gain full support for the war effort. In the United States, the antiwar movement also appealed to patriotism, arguing in speeches and images that to be true to American values and ideals, the public should oppose the war and join the struggle for peace. The pictures in this essay illustrate the varieties of appeals for public support made by all the governments and, in the United States, ordinary citizens who supported or opposed the war.

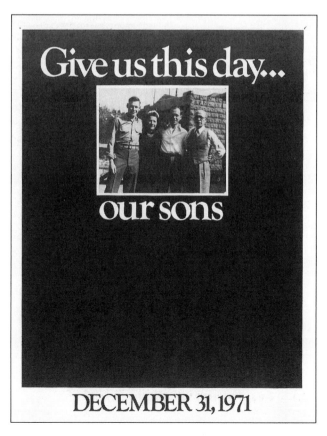

In 1971, a coalition of 30 advertising agencies joined forces in the Committee to Help Unsell the War. Their work was highly professional. Here are two examples: A play on the familiar military recruiting poster shows a wounded Uncle Sam saying "I Want Out" (left); "Give Us This Day" (right) alludes to the Lord's Prayer.

These stamps, issued by the North Vietnamese government, had two goals: to inspire people and to make the firepower of the United States seem less awesome. Peasants shoot down planes and helicopters and prepare booby-traps with "punji sticks" (sharp, poisoned sticks) against American soldiers. Two of the stamps commemorate particular struggles in the south: one in Tay Ninh province (bottom left), the other in Cu Chi (bottom center), where local guerrillas had built an extensive underground tunnel network from which they fought first the French and later the Americans.

The antiwar movement placed its advertisements where it hoped soldiers would see them. This ad appeared in *Playboy* magazine in February 1971. Through the powerful image of a flag-draped coffin and the statistics of casualties, it appeals to veterans and citizens to join in support of Vietnam Veterans Against the War.

The sense that the war against the United States had widespread international support was important in the effort of the North Vietnamese government to mobilize their population. This poster shows the peoples of the Third World responding to the raised weapon of the Vietnamese soldier in the foreground.

The antiwar movement used older and more familiar images as well. For example, recalling baseball trading cards, "Amerika Outlaw Trading Cards" featured the Berrigan Brothers, both Roman Catholic priests, whose campaign against the draft had led to their arrest and imprisonment. The figure of Christ stands behind them, indicating whom the Berrigans took to be the justification for their civil disobedience.

SOCIAL DEVIANTS

THE BERRIGAN BROS. Ω

Daniel and Phillip Berrigan, both Roman Catholic priests, are presently in Federal prison for willful destruction of Selective Service records.

Both were among the earliest and most vociferous members of the anti-war, anti-draft movement and have participated extensively in militant actions against draft boards around the country. Among their actions were a public burning of draft-board records and the pouring of gallons of duck's blood over SS files in a Balti-more-area induction center.

Amerikan Outlaw Trading Cards

Looking a good deal like the advertisements that appear at the back of comic books or men's magazines, this "Fed Up With the Army, Navy, Marines" box makes a direct appeal to soldiers to desert.

Rewriting the usual notations on a dollar bill to list the Vietnamese and American casualties, imagining a Russian spelling of America, and giving the unit of currency in terms of death spun a strong antiwar message in this 1970 parody.

Much like the dollar bill seen above, this check to be drawn on the "Bank of Amerika" mocks items, such as bank checks, familiar to most Americans.

A Viet-Nam soldier prepares to bury his infant son, slain by the Viet Cong

'liberation' or conquest?

THE STRUGGLE IN SOUTH VIETNAM

U.S. government efforts to explain the war to the American people made extensive use of photographs. The cover of this pamphlet on the war illustrates the question of whether the war was for liberation or conquest, with a picture of a South Vietnamese soldier weeping as he prepares to bury his dead baby.

1969

Committee for Cultural Relations with Foreign Countries
HANOI–D. R. VIETNAM

The North Vietnamese had their own versions of calendar girls. This joyous guerrilla from Cu Chi, an area of intense fighting and high casualties, was intended to raise morale on the home front.

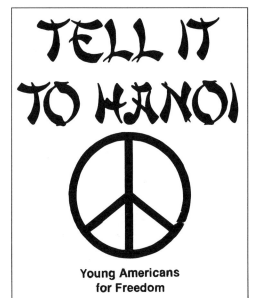

TELL IT TO HANOI

Young Americans for Freedom

Pro-war American groups, such as the Young Americans for Freedom, hoped to turn popular anti-war symbols against the antiwar movement. This poster, with its imitation Chinese calligraphy, the peace symbol, and the slogan "Tell it to Hanoi" is itself an argument: it is Hanoi, not the United States, that blocks the road to peace.

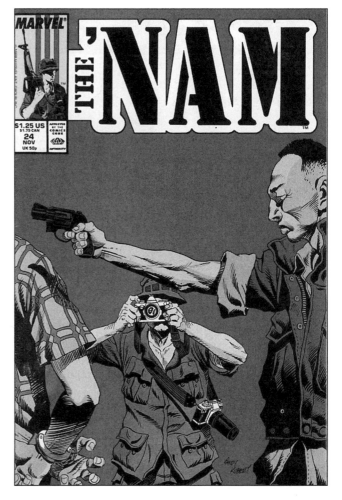

The war continued to be sold long after it ended in 1975. In the mid-1980s comic book *The 'Nam*, the image of the guerrilla fighter was often taken away from the Viet Cong and assigned to an American. The cover above shows a blindfolded American prisoner with a rope around his neck. It underlines Viet Cong brutality to American troops, as opposed to familiar images of Vietnamese being brutalized by American or South Vietnamese troops. The cover at the right plays off one of the war's most shocking photographs, of a Republic of South Vietnam army officer shooting an unarmed Viet Cong prisoner. By focusing on the photographer, the image implies the complicity of the press in making the war unpopular at home.

Maintaining military morale was no less important to the war effort than civilian mobilization. As in earlier American wars, well-known stars, like Bob Hope, entertained the troops. On Christmas Eve, 1965, General Westmoreland formally thanked Bob Hope for his contribution to troop morale.

The North Vietnamese similarly sought to circulate well-known photographic images in other forms. The news photograph of an armed woman guarding an American pilot whose plane had crashed had obvious appeal: the woman looks serious and determined; the prisoner's head is bowed, his hands tied. Thus a small Asian woman has power over a tall white man: Asia has power over America. The photograph was made into a stamp that both commemorated the deed and circulated the image throughout North Vietnam.

VIET-NAM
MAY
JUNE
JULY
AUGUST
SEPTEMBER
NOVEMBER
DECEMBER
JANUARY
FEBUARY
545
25-24
HOME

Chapter 5

Going to War

The war in Vietnam was not an abstraction for the millions of men and women, Vietnamese and American, who were caught up in it. Nor was there a single experience of the war. The impact of the war on an individual soldier during his one-year tour of duty depended on whether he was in a combat or a support unit; in which part of the country he served and in what year; whether he enlisted or was drafted; whether he was in the Marines, the Air Force, or the Infantry. The war in the Mekong Delta was not the same as the war in the highlands. Serving time in Saigon or a major base camp was vastly different from time on a fire base or on patrol in the countryside. Many soldiers never saw the enemy; others fought full-scale conventional battles against readily identified enemy units.

From 1965 to 1969, ground combat increased sharply as the American military pursued a policy of "attrition," which sought to increase the "body count" of enemy dead rather than attempt to secure territory. Small units were frequently sent on patrol in order to attract enemy fire; a single enemy sniper could invite a full scale air attack. Thus ground combat units often felt they served as bait—and suffered a similar fate. As the war dragged on, there was a noticeable deterioration of the U.S. military in Vietnam, with increased levels of drug use, desertion, racial disturbances, small mutinies, and attacks by soldiers against their officers and noncommissioned officers (known as "fragging" because a fragmentation grenade was the weapon of choice).

Soldiers at War

Most young American men got their introduction to the Vietnam War by way of their draft notice. Once an American male turned 18 years of age his local draft board was obliged to send him an Order to Report for Induction unless he applied for exemption according to one of these categories: college student, married, a

An American soldier's tour of duty in Vietnam was 365 days, and one's time there was called "in country." Almost everyone counted the days they had left. This Sky Trooper from the 1st Cavalry Division (Airmobile) used his helmet as a calendar; to be "short" meant you were almost home free.

conscientious objector, homosexual, felon, or having medical or mental problems.

The President of the United States,

To _____

GREETINGS:

You are hereby ordered for induction into the Armed Forces of the United States, and to report at

_____ on

_____ at _____

for forwarding to an Armed Forces Induction Station.

IMPORTANT NOTICE

If you are so far from your own local board that reporting in compliance with this Order will be serious hardship, go immediately to any local board and make written request for transfer of your delivery for induction, taking this Order.

IF YOU HAVE HAD PREVIOUS MILITARY SERVICE, OR ARE NOW A MEMBER OF THE NATIONAL GUARD, OR A RESERVE COMPONENT OF THE ARMED FORCES, BRING EVIDENCE WITH YOU. IF YOU WEAR GLASSES, BRING THEM. IF MARRIED, BRING PROOF OF YOUR MARRIAGE. IF YOU HAVE ANY PHYSICAL OR MENTAL CONDITION WHICH, IN YOUR OPINION, MAY DISQUALIFY YOU FOR SERVICE IN THE ARMED FORCES, BRING A PHYSICIAN'S CERTIFICATE DESCRIBING THAT CONDITION, IF NOT ALREADY FURNISHED TO YOUR LOCAL BOARD.

Bring your Social Security Account Number Card. If you do not have one, apply at nearest Social Security Administration Office. If you have life insurance, bring a record of the insurance company's address and your policy number. Bring enough clean clothes for 3 days. Bring enough money to last 1 month for personal purchases.

The Local Board will furnish transportation, and meals and lodging when necessary, from the place of reporting to the induction station where you will be examined. If found qualified, you will be inducted into the Armed Forces. If found not qualified, return transportation and meals and lodging, when necessary, will be furnished to the place of reporting.

You may be found not qualified for induction. Keep this in mind in arranging your affairs, to prevent any undue hardships if you are not inducted. If employed, inform your employer of this

[The enemy's] guerrilla force is declining at a steady rate.
—General William Westmoreland, from a November 1967 speech

Vietnam--Place and People

The Place:

+++ Is in southeast corner of Asia, bounded by Laos, Cambodia, and South China Sea.

+++ In shape, long and narrow. In size, about the same area as the state of Washington.

+++ Geography: central highland comprises two-thirds of country, with chain of mountains, dense jungles, some open forests. Narrow coastal plain runs from northern tip almost to Saigon, is very level with numerous beaches, backed by a narrow piedmont of open hills. Delta, in south, takes 25 per cent of land mass, has more than 50 per cent of population. Yields immense rice crop. Has more than 3,500 miles of navigable rivers and canals.

+++ Climate is tropical, monsoonal, with hot-dry, hot-wet seasons varying through country.

The People:

+++ Number about 15.5 million, 85 per cent being ethnic Vietnamese. About one million Chinese, half-million Cambodians, 800,000 Montagnards (mountain tribal groups) make up most of remainder. Eighty per cent of population are farmers. About half of people are concentrated in the area from just north of Saigon south through the delta.

+++ Worship ancestors, venerate elders, hold family as keystone of society. They are quieter, less excitable than Westerners, place high value on harmony, good manners, tradition.

+++ Are proud, valiant, have stood up bravely under communist harassment 12 years, longer than any other nation.

The Enemy

The Enemy:

+++ Is communist North Vietnam and its southern arm, Viet Cong (Vietnamese communist or "Viet Red").

+++ Controls, directs, supplies entire effort to conquer Republic of Vietnam through COSVN (Central Office for South Vietnam), which heads military, political efforts of North Vietnam in South Vietnam, closely resembles government structure, reaches into every district.

+++ Trains military, political cadres, terrorists, spies, saboteurs, providing most of VC leadership. These have infiltrated in increasing numbers since 1956.

+++ Uses systematic terrorism, assassination to wreck economy, destroy fabric of government of 2,600 villages. In past five years communists have assassinated, beheaded or kidnaped 2,000 village chiefs, have driven away able-bodied men, have deluded or terrorized many citizens into cooperating.

+++ Still failing to win, in 1965 Hanoi began sending regular units of North Vietnamese Army to south. Backbone of communist military in South Vietnam is VC "main force" and NVA units, of about 112,000. VC guerrillas number 113,000, political cadres 39,000, combat support 18,000. (Estimates are as of summer 1966.)

+++ Estimated average of at least 5,000 men infiltrated South Vietnam monthly during first seven months of 1966, plus supplies, by land and sea from north. Arms are from China, Russia, Red satellites.

+++ In first half of 1966, however, 10,000 VC and NVA soldiers and sympathizers turned themselves in to South Vietnam government under Chieu Hoi (open arms) program.

Navy—Pearl Harbor

ready reference facts on

SOUTH VIETNAM

Office of Information
Military Assistance Command, Vietnam
APO San Francisco 96243

possibility. Your employer can then be prepared to continue your employment if you are not inducted. To protect your right to return to your job if you are not inducted, you must report for work as soon as possible after the completion of your induction examination. You may jeopardize your re-employment rights if you do not report to work at the beginning of your next regularly scheduled working period after you have returned to your place of employment.

Willful failure to report at the place and hour of the day named in this Order subjects the violator to fine and imprisonment. Bring this Order with you when you report.

When the war began, and perhaps for much longer, few Americans knew much about Vietnam, not even where it was. The military gave soldiers what it felt were the most essential facts, including the warning that Vietnamese were "quieter" than Westerners and cared a lot about "good manners." Its description of Vietnam's history of resistance to outside aggression omitted any reference to the Chinese, French, or Japanese and failed to note that the communists involved were themselves Vietnamese.

Larry Rottman, a poet and combat veteran, indicates in this poem, whose title is the mailing address of the 25th Infantry Division in Vietnam, what the letters soldiers wrote home concealed and why concealment was necessary.

APO 96225

A young man once went off to war in a far country,
and when he had time, he wrote home and said,
"Dear Mom, sure rains a lot here."

But his mother—reading between the lines as mothers
   always do—wrote back,
"We're quite concerned. Tell us what it's really like."

And the young man responded,
"Wow! You ought to see the funny monkeys."

To which the mother replied,
"Don't hold back. How is it there?"

And the young man wrote,
"The sunsets here are spectacular!"

In her next letter, the mother pleaded,
"Son, we want you to tell us everything. Everything!"

So the next time he wrote, the young man said,
"Today I killed a man. Yesterday, I helped drop napalm
    on women and children."

And the father wrote back,
"Please don't write such depressing letters. You're
    upsetting your mother."

So, after a while,
the young man wrote,
"Dear Mom, sure rains a lot."

**Those who fought with the National Liberation Front and the
North Vietnamese did so under very different conditions
from those of the American forces. Their war is recorded in
letters and diaries found on the bodies of the dead or taken
from those who surrendered. Many diary entries included
poems, such as this one written by Duc Thanh, entitled "In
the Forest of the Night."**

Many days and months have passed
And still I fight.
Living with difficulty and hardship
Is how the soldier of liberation is trained.
We must learn to live with bombs
Shaking the sky
And the heavy smell of gun powder.
My life is hard and miserable, my friends.
I am the son of the Vietnamese,
Under siege for a hundred years
By the French and the Americans.
I roll in the dust. I sleep in a bed of thorns
To bring peace to my country.

Long nights and days I don't eat or sleep.
My body turns to bones.
Bombs pour down on me. . . .
Oh friends, my mother is old.
She waits for me in our village.
Every night she waits to see me return
So she can finally close her eyes.
Day and night our village is bombed.
I'm afraid she will die before seeing me again.

The political officials of the National Liberation Front were not exempt from the dangers of the battlefront. Truong Nhu Tang, whose memories of meeting Ho Chi Minh appeared in Chapter 2, describes the conditions under which he lived for six years.

We lived like hunted animals, an existence that demanded constant physical and mental alertness. . . . Ready to move at any instant, we kept our personal encumbrances to a minimum. Two pairs of black pajamas, a couple of pair of underpants, a mosquito net, and a few square yards of light nylon (handy as a raincoat or roof) were all that a guerrilla owned. The fighters, of course, carried weapons and ammunition in addition, as well as "elephant's intestines," our term for the long tubes of rolled cotton that could be filled with rice and slung across the back.

In addition to rice, each man's personal larder was rounded out by a small hunk of salt, a piece of monosodium glutamate, and perhaps a little dried fish or meat. The rice ration for both leaders and fighters was twenty kilos [44 pounds] a month. Eaten twice a day, at about nine in the morning and four in the afternoon, the ration did not go far. But by and large it was our entire diet, a nutritional intake that left us all in a state of semistarvation.

Truong describes the complicated routes through which such items as sugar, tobacco, salt, soap, etc. were supplied and the way the supply system was transformed in 1970 when it seemed the whole country was flooded with Japanese motorbikes.

In one way or another, these bikes made their way out from the cities and into the hands of even the most remote country people, who would then smuggle them to the guerrillas. Quite often the peasants would get their bikes from the local Saigon army forces. . . . Eventually, our Finance Department was able to set up regular supply channels directly between [the ARVN's 5th and 18th Divisions] and the Front in weapons and ammunition as well. . . . More than a few American soldiers were killed with . . . mines bought from their ARVN comrades. . . . But neither these supply sources nor the materiel flowing down from the North along the Ho Chi Minh Trail alleviated the chronic malnutrition or the tropical diseases that battened on the weakened men. In the jungle the prime enemy was not the Americans or the *nguy* ("puppets," our term for the Saigon government and its troops) but malaria. . . . For each of my years in the jungle, I spent approximately two months in the hospital, battling the high fevers and general debility of the disease.

But for all the privations and hardships, nothing the guerrillas had to endure compared with the stark terrorization of the B-52 bombardments. . . . From a kilometer away, the sonic roar of the B-52 explosions tore eardrums, leaving many of the jungle dwellers permanently deaf. From a kilometer, the shock waves knocked their victims senseless. Any hit within a half kilometer would collapse the walls of an unreinforced bunker, burying alive the people cowering inside. Seen up close, the bomb craters were gigantic—thirty feet across and nearly as deep. . . . [Aided by advance intelligence, military and civilian leaders were generally able to survive the raids in bunkers or by evacuating the targeted area.] Hours later we would return to find . . . that there was nothing left. It was as if an enormous scythe had swept through the jungle, felling the giant . . . trees like grass in its way, shredding them into a million splinters. . . . It was not just that things were destroyed; in some awesome way they had ceased to exist. You

The North Vietnamese moved supplies as well as troops from north to
south over an intricate network of
trails and roads. Developed initially
during the war against the French,
the trails expanded over the 10 years
of the American war. By 1967,
20,000 or more North Vietnamese
troops moved south over the Ho Chi
Minh trail each month despite non-
stop U.S. bombing.

would come back to where your lean-to and bunker had been,
your home, and there would simply be nothing there, just an
unrecognizable landscape gouged by an immense crater. . . .

The first few times I experienced a B-52 attack it seemed, as I
strained to press myself into the bunker floor, that I had been
caught in the Apocalypse. The terror was complete. One lost control of bodily functions as the mind screamed incomprehensible
orders to get out. . . .

Sooner or later, though, the shock of bombardments wore off,
giving way to a sense of abject fatalism. . . . But even the most
philosophical of fatalists were worn to the breaking point after
several years of dodging and burrowing away from the rain of
high explosives. During the most intense periods we came under
attack every day for weeks running.

**In contrast to the light equipment of the guerrillas, the nov-
elist and combat veteran Tim O'Brien lists the things American troops carried.**

What they carried was partly a function of rank, partly of field
specialty.

As a first lieutenant and platoon leader, Jimmy Cross carried a
compass, maps, code books, binoculars and a .45-caliber pistol
that weighed 2.9 pounds fully loaded. He carried a strobe light
and the responsibility for the lives of his men.

As an RTO [Radio Telephone Operator], Mitchell Sanders carried the PRC-25 radio, a killer, 26 pounds with its battery.

As a medic, Rat Kiley carried a canvas satchel filled with morphine and plasma and malaria tablets and surgical tape and comic books and all the things a medic must carry, including M&Ms [the candy] for especially bad wounds, for a total weight of nearly 20 pounds.

As a big man, therefore a machine gunner, Henry Dobbins carried the M-60, which weighed 23 pounds unloaded but which was almost always loaded. In addition, Dobbins carried between 10 and 15 pounds of ammunition draped in belts across his chest and shoulders.

A marine walks through a gully staked with "punji" sticks—sharpened pieces of wood with homemade toxins on the tips. North Vietnamese and NLF main forces were increasingly well supplied as the war continued. By 1972, the North Vietnamese were able to mount a full-scale tank attack. Local guerrilla forces, however, continued to rely on these low-tech solutions to high-tech war.

As PFCs Spec 4s, most of them were common grunts and carried the standard M-16 gas-operated assault rifle. The weapon weighed 7.5 pounds unloaded, 8.2 pounds with its full 20-round magazine. Depending on numerous factors, such as topography and psychology, the riflemen carried anywhere from 12 to 20 magazines, usually in both bandoliers, adding on another 8.4 pounds at minimum, 14 pounds at maximum. When it was available, they also carried M-16 maintenance gear-rods and steel brushes and swabs and tubes of LSA oil—all of which weighed about a pound. Among the grunts, some carried the M-79 grenade launcher, 5.9 pounds unloaded, a reasonably light weapon except for the ammunition, which was heavy. A single round weighed 10 ounces. The typical load was 25 rounds. But Ted Lavender, who was scared, carried 34 rounds when he was shot and killed outside Than Khe, and he went down under an exceptional burden, more than 20 pounds of ammunition, plus the flak jacket and helmet and rations and water and toilet paper and tranquilizers and all the rest, plus the unweighed fear. . . .

In addition to the three standard weapons—the M-60s, M-16, and M-79—they carried whatever presented itself, or whatever seemed appropriate to staying alive. They carried catch-as-catch-can. At various times, in various situations, they carried M-14s and CAR-15s and Swedish Ks and grease guns and captured AK-47s and Chi-coms and RPGs and Simonov carbines and black market Uzis and .38-caliber Smith & Wesson handguns and 66mm LAWs and shotguns and silencers and blackjacks and bayonets and C-4 plastic explosives. . . . Every third or fourth man carried a Claymore antipersonnel mine—3.5 pounds with its firing device. They all carried fragmentation grenades—14 ounces each. They all carried at least one M-18 colored smoke grenade—24 ounces. Some carried CS or tear gas grenades. Some carried white phosphorous grenades. They carried all they could bear, and then some, including a silent awe for the terrible power of the things they carried.

An infantry squad leader shouts instructions to his squad. He carries the gear of war, and in addition, perhaps as a hope rather than a contradiction, a large peace medallion.

Other Voices

There was a dramatic disconnection between what the soldiers were officially told they were doing in Vietnam and what they were actually doing. The discrepancy is vividly illustrated by comparing the language of military citations and awards with the memories of the soldiers who

received them. John J. Fitzgerald—one of the authors of this book—was awarded the Bronze Star for Valor. The official citation stated

HEADQUARTERS
25TH INFANTRY DIVISION
APO San Francisco 96225
GENERAL ORDERS 23 July 1966
NUMBER 614
AWARD OF THE BRONZE STAR MEDAL FOR HEROISM
TC 320. The following AWARDS are announced.
FITZGERALD, JOHN J. 05324915 ILT INF USA
Co B, 4th Bn, 9th Inf, 25th Inf Div
Awarded: Bronze Star Medal with "V" Device
Date action: 26 June 1966
Theater: Republic of Vietnam
Reason: For heroism in connection with military operations against a hostile force.

Lieutenant Fitzgerald distinguished himself by heroic actions on 26 June 1966, in the Republic of Vietnam. On this date, he was serving as platoon leader of a platoon size search and destroy operation against the Viet Cong. At approximately 1615 hours, Lieutenant Fitzgerald received a call from one of his fire team leaders that his squad was engaged with the Viet Cong and needed reinforcements, immediately he summoned his only available squad and personally led them approximately 600 meters to his fire team leader's position. Under heavy machine gun and automatic weapons fire, Lieutenant Fitzgerald personally led the assault on the enemy's position. He directed the maneuver of his elements and continued moving forward while firing and throwing hand grenades until he was seriously wounded and unable to continue the advance. From his position approximately ten meters from the enemy, he continued to lead the attack and function as a platoon leader even though weakened by loss of a considerable amount of blood. He refused medical treatment until all the other wounded men had been treated, and was one of the last men evacuated. By his actions, Lieutenant Fitzgerald instilled in his men a will to fight until the enemy fire was silenced and evacuation of the wounded could be affected. Lieutenant Fitzgerald's outstanding display of aggressiveness, devotion to duty, and personal bravery is in keeping with the highest standards of the military service and reflects great credit upon himself, his unit, and the 25th Infantry Division of the United States Army.

Authority: By direction of the President under the provisions of Executive Order 11046, 24 August 1962, and USARV message 16695, 1 July 1966.
FOR THE COMMANDER:
OFFICIAL: THOMAS W. MELLEN
Colonel, GS; Chief of Staff
/s//
HERBERT L. FORSYTHE LTC, AGC
Adjutant General
HEADQUARTERS DIVISION 1LT

But John Fitzgerald felt differently:

What I still vividly remember of 26 June 1966 is best described without rhetoric or heroics. I was awarded the Bronze Star with "V" device. The "V" stand for Valor.

I was nominated for the Bronze Star and the Purple Heart. Since I left the military after my wounds healed, I never wore the medals on my uniform. I keep them in the box in which they came. I cite the two medals in my resumé and I used them to establish my credentials when I was speaking out against the war.

I served in Vietnam as an Infantry Platoon Leader. I ran 1st Platoon of B Company of the 4th Battalion, 9th Infantry. I served in the 25th Infantry Division and our base camp was in Cu Chi, Republic of Vietnam.

On the 26th of June, 1966, my platoon and I had been in country since the 1st of May. We were relatively seasoned soldiers, but we had not seen much combat up until then. I was working with a reinforced platoon and we were looking for a sniper and/or snipers known to be located in the area outside of our perimeter. We now know that there was a vast tunnel complex in Cu Chi and that there many National Liberation Front guerillas stationed there.

My mission was to search for and destroy the enemy. I was also told to destroy any unexploded ordnance we might find in the area. The Air Force had earlier dropped some bombs out there and they missed the target. As a result, they left some "dud" bombs in the vicinity and these could be used by the "enemy" to make land mines for use against us.

As we moved through the area we were supposed to search, we drew some small arms fire from the sniper or snipers. We found one 100 pound bomb and blew it up. I then had my platoon break down into three search groups to check out the remaining area. I

A wounded John J. Fitzgerald receives his Bronze Star. He wore it that day for the first and last time.

kept one squad in reserve for use in a counter-ambush, if needed. One of the squads came upon a group of "enemy" and opened up on them. They had somehow come in from behind on them and they had "ambushed" them. Charles Brown fired at them with his M-60 machine-gun. He hit them. This fire team then moved in to investigate. They called on the radio to report what happened and I remember telling them to be careful. They were then ambushed by other "enemy" elements and I moved out to their location with my reserve squad and we countered the counterambush. As we moved out, we did reconnaissance by fire in case there were some non-friendlies in the bushes waiting for us. I remember feeling a tremendous adrenaline rush as we moved out.

When we got to the ambush site, I realized I was out of ammunition and ducked behind a tree for some cover and started to reload my M-16. Then I got hit. My arm felt like it had been punched and I looked down and saw a small hole through my tattoo and felt my arm dangling. I did not feel pain. I guess I was in shock. There was some firing and then everything was silent. I can remember giving some orders about getting the wounded out. And I started walking back to my earlier location. When I got there I saw Brown's body and I told the medic to give him mouth to mouth resuscitation. He told me that he was dead. I went out on the helicopter that took Brown's body out. When I got to the medical area I was still walking but I must have been in shock. I had a huge exit wound and most of my arm and shoulder were torn up. I could not see that but I remember noticing the reaction of people to me. They looked horrified. They cut my boot laces off and slit up my uniform. I remember being very thirsty and I still recall the last words of the doctor when they were giving me anesthesia. I was holding my breath and he said, "Don't fight it."

After I was able to write up what I could understand of the situation, the Company Commander must have interviewed some

The U.S. government distributed to incoming U.S. troops simple line drawings of guerrilla hideouts. The illustrations make simple what was actually very difficult: how to distinguish between an ordinary peasant family's bomb shelter or storage area and an NLF village defense structure. Often they were one and the same.

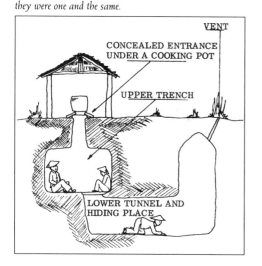

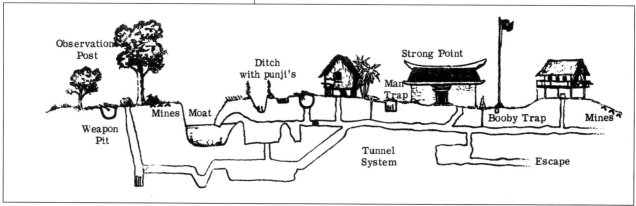

others and he pieced together the story that appears in the Bronze Star citation. I don't recall any enemy machine-gun fire. I later was told that the entire company was listening to our progress on the radio back in base camp. The firing of weapons was probably largely our own. It must have sounded like quite an adventure.

In truth, it was a small action in the context of a larger war. I do not think what I did was particularly heroic or valorous. It was our job and we were doing it. I know my happiest moment in Vietnam was when I was hit, because I "knew" I was homeward bound. I have never wanted to be out of a place more than Vietnam. The place filled me with dread and I have never known the kind of fear I felt there any place else.

Sometimes the damage American troops caused was almost casual. Michael Casey, a Vietnam veteran, tells the story of what armored personnel carriers (called "tracks" because of metal cleats on which they moved)—all bearing affectionate nicknames—could do to a farmer's rice fields.

A Bummer

We were going single file
Through his rice paddies
And the farmer
Started hitting the lead track
With a rake
He wouldn't stop
The TC [tank commander] went to talk to him
And the farmer
Tried to hit him too
So the tracks went sideways
Side by side
Through the guy's fields
Instead of single file
Hard On, Proud Mary
Bummer, Wallace, Rosemary's Baby
The Rutgers Road Runner
And
Go Get Em-Done Got Em
Went side by side
Through the fields
If you have a farm in Vietnam
And a house in hell
Sell the farm
And go home

Hoang Thi Ai worked in a clinic in North Vietnam treating those wounded by the bombing. In this interview, she tells of the challenges of working in a North Vietnamese clinic.

We had practically no medicine, just some penicillin and streptomycin. For napalm [jellied gasoline dropped by bombs to create fire] victims we had only a burn spray. We sprayed their bodies and took them to the hospital. But here they dropped a lot of fragmentation bombs to kill the people. We could only bandage them and bring them to the hospital. We carried the wounded on bamboo stretchers, on foot through the fields, thirty kilometers. You couldn't use the road because of the airplanes.

Lieutenant Frances Crumpton and Nurse Nangnoi Thongkin comfort a wounded American soldier in a Navy hospital in Saigon. There were 7,465 women serving in the military in Vietnam; 80 percent were nurses.

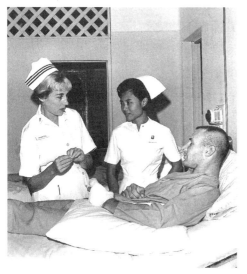

A Japanese war correspondent recounts similar events.

The five APC tanks drove right into the golden waves of rice paddies. The ripe ears of rice, now ready to be harvested, were mercilessly trodden and kneaded in the muddy field under the caterpillars as they took their capricious ways all over the paddies. They did not even have the kindness to make each tank follow the wake of the preceding one. The seed beds of rice plants, and the newly planted paddies—all these were nothing in their eyes.

The tanks chose their respective routes, as sports cars driven for fun, each of them leaving new deep ruts in the rice paddies. In the heart of American soldiers, there was a hopeless lack of an element common to rice-cultivating peoples. This lack makes it impossible for them to understand the mind of these peasants. The gulf lying between the two makes one despair.

Most of the peasants reaping rice were old people, women and children. As was always the case, they never turned their eyes toward the tanks. They continued their work, without uttering a word.

Nurses and medical personnel, although not directly involved in the fighting, encountered its consequences in the most painful way. Some 10,000 women served in Vietnam as members of the Women's Army Corps (WACS), Marines, and civilians with the Red Cross, the United Service Organization (USO), the Peace Corps, and religious organizations. The largest group was nurses. Christine McGinley Schneider served with the 95th Evacuation Hospital, Da Nang, from June 1970 to June 1971. In an interview, she recounted the following.

I don't know how to describe it. I had worked a year in the emergency room on the jail ward, but nothing could prepare you for the horrible things you saw. . . .You just get thrown into it. The first day they had a mass casualty, and they got as many doctors, nurses, and corpsmen as they could down there. It was just incredible; these big Chinook helicopters came in, and the corpsmen went out and got all these guys. I remember one of the nurses saying, "You take him." I'll never forget him because he was my first one. Everybody was bad, but they were alive. . . . He was a really good-looking boy—Jimmy was his name—with blond hair, and half of his face had been blown away, and the first thing the nurse said to me was "Cut off all of his clothes." They give you these

A North Vietnamese army field hospital operates in deep trenches to protect doctors and patients from constant bombing.

huge scissors to cut off the clothes, and I was trying to comfort him. . . . He was wide awake even though half his face was gone, and he was scared. I remember cutting off all his clothes and the horror of taking off one of his boots and his foot still being in the boot. . . . I remember that nurse saying, "Draw four tubes of blood, type-cross him, and get it over to the lab right away." I remember drawing the blood, but he begged me not to leave. . . . After I drew the blood he said, "Please don't leave me." I said, "I just have to run across the hall to the lab. I promise I'll be right back." I was right back, and he had died in the time that I had left him alone. . . . And I never forgot that; I never again left anyone, because you realize that when they say that, it's like they know that they are going.

There was a daily level of violence in Vietnam quite apart
from such infamous incidents such as the My Lai massacre,
in which more than 400 unarmed villagers were killed by

American troops. The official rules did not seem to apply, as described in the testimony of David Bressem, an army helicopter pilot, before an ad hoc congressional committee chaired by Representative Ron Dellums of California, one of the most vocal critics of the war. The hearings were the direct result of the efforts of veterans to educate the public on the nature of the war in Vietnam and to demonstrate that massacres and other atrocities were the consequence of U.S. government policies rather than isolated acts of individual soldiers. Veterans held their own Citizens' Commissions of

Only 16 miles from Saigon, the U.S. 199th Light Infantry Brigade begins a sweep through a pineapple plantation. Soldiers testified about what took place on search and destroy missions like this one before the Dellums Committee, which sought to educate the public about the atrocities of the war.

About 19 million gallons of three toxic herbicides were sprayed over large areas of South Vietnam from 1961 to 1970. Herbicides were used to clear jungle hiding places and destroy food crops that might feed enemy troops, although it also harmed crops planted by ordinary peasants. The most effective of the herbicides was Agent Orange, which was later discovered to cause severe health problems to both the Vietnamese receiving it and the Americans who sprayed it.

Inquiry in a number of different cities from March through December 1970. Although the panel lacked official committee status, Dellums was able to hold the hearings in the House Caucus Room and received considerable publicity.

Anyone taking evasive action could be fired upon. Evasive action was never explained to me. It normally entailed someone running or trying to evade a helicopter or any fire. My unit . . . had installed MP sirens on the helicopter and we used these for psychological effect, to intimidate the people. There is one incident I recall where we flew over a large rice paddy, and there were some people working in the rice paddy, making a dozen or fifteen individuals, and we passed a couple of times over their heads and they didn't take any action, they were obviously nervous, but they didn't try to hide or anything. So we then hovered a few feet off the ground among them with the two helicopters, turned on the police sirens and when they heard the police sirens, they started to disperse and we opened up on them and just shot them all down.

The Condition of the Army

By 1971, the pressures of the Vietnam war threatened a crisis in the army itself, as B. Drummond Ayers Jr., reported in the *New York Times* in the spring of 1971.

Agent Orange

In 1979, New York Times *reporter Richard Severo exposed the effects of Agent Orange. Agent Orange is a powerful herbicide and defoliant containing the poisonous chemical dioxin. It was sprayed by low-flying planes to deprive enemy troops of foliage cover. In 1989 Severo wrote* The Wages of War, *chronicling the difficulty veterans had in getting the U.S. government to acknowledge their complaints and symptoms.*

Uncovering Agent Orange was a sobering and disillusioning experience. I realized that people in the government had lied to us about the need to go to Vietnam. It was a huge mistake, but the bigger mistake was that they also turned their backs on all the people who had been conscripted to fight that war. . . . In my research, I randomly interviewed veterans who had reported strange symptoms. Guys were telling me that they couldn't even drink a beer without getting sick or having huge lumps on their arms. After speaking to 150 of them I took all my findings to the Veterans Administration, which told me that the vets were just "goldbrickers" who wanted something for nothing. . . . I wanted to see a change in the Pentagon, but I am not sure I made anything happen. I don't see that anything has changed.

Son Chan Valley, Vietnam

**"I'M SORRY SIR,
BUT MY MEN REFUSE TO GO....
WE CANNOT MOVE OUT"**

Lieutenant in command of Company A

USSF
UNITED STATES SERVICEMEN'S FUND
94 SCHOOL ST., CAMBRIDGE, MASS. 02138

THE END

The poster, produced by the United States Servicemen's Fund, an antiwar organization, celebrates the small mutinies that increasingly plagued the military as the war dragged on.

The bitter Vietnam experience has left the United States Army with a crisis in morale and discipline as serious as any its oldest and toughest soldiers can remember.

At fire bases around Saigon, in the guard towers at the Berlin Wall, on the parade ground at Ft. Benning, Ga., there is concern that the men in the ranks no longer have the esprit necessary to make first-class fighters.

The men themselves are fed up with the war and the draft, questioning orders, deserting, subverting, smoking marijuana, shooting heroin, stealing from their buddies, hurling racial epithets and rocks at their brothers.

Their leaders, trained to handle a different sort of crisis, often seem as bewildered as the rawest recruits, compromising, innovating, ordering strategic retreats from tradition, tossing out the training manual—all with uncharacteristic pliability.

The desertion rate soars, so they do away with bed checks and permit psychedelic posters on barracks walls. . . . The troops refuse to advance, so they talk it over with them and try to find another way. . . .

Over the last 12 months, 177 of every 1,000 American soldiers have been listed as "absent without leave," some three or four times. And 74 out of every 1,000 men have stayed away a month or more and thus have been classified as deserters.

These rates represent roughly a three-fold increase over the desertion and absenteeism rates recorded five years or so ago when the Army was just beginning its buildup in Vietnam and the war was less a political issue. . . .

Medical tests given men leaving Vietnam indicate that about four of every hundred are drug users. . . . "The Vietnam drug situation is extremely serious," says Brig. Gen. Robert G. Gard, Jr., a Pentagon specialist in disciplinary problems. "The testing, thus far, has been spotty. And we even have cases of testers—they're mostly soldiers themselves—falsifying the test results for their buddies. . . .

Racial tensions have so polarized whites and blacks in many units that fights break out periodically in bunk areas and latrines. In mess halls, blacks and whites frequently sit down at separate tables, the blacks greeting each other with upthrust black power salutes and elaborate "dap" hand shakes. . . .

Court-martial convictions for insubordination, mutiny and refusal to obey orders climbed from 230 in 1968 to 294 in 1969 to 331 last year. This year convictions may exceed 450.

These figures represent only the extreme cases. No statistics are kept on the less serious incidents which occur almost daily in many units. . . .

"Working it out" . . . started in Vietnam, where the practice continues. The procedure is simple and has even been filmed by television news crews.

A unit or man refuses to advance or take an order. Everybody—including officers and sergeants—sits down and talks. A safer route or alternative job is agreed upon.

Officers and sergeants in Vietnam who refuse to participate in these discussions run the risk of being "fragged" by a hand grenade tossed into their bunk by one of their own men.

In 1969 there were 126 "actual" or "possible" fraggings. The count rose to 271 last year, and this year it probably will exceed 425. Seventy-eight men have been killed and more than 600 wounded.

Chapter 6

A People Divided

The United States as a whole was divided by the war. And so was the military in the field. Most people think of the antiwar movement mainly in terms of angry student demonstrations. Of perhaps greater importance were two other sources of opposition: the poor and minorities who, lacking educational deferments, sympathetic draft boards, and accommodating doctors were disproportionately called upon to serve in the military and, as the war went on, some of the very men who were fighting it.

The African-American Community

The civil rights movement, which had consumed the attention of the United States from the early 1960s on, overlapped with the antiwar movement and people were quick to connect the two. The war diverted funds and energy from President Johnson's war against poverty; more lethally, the growing need for manpower pulled young African American men into the ranks of the military, often to their death, in a cause many African Americans thought dubious at best.

Of the 11 million Americans who served in the military in the Vietnam era, some 2 million of them in Vietnam itself, 600,000 young men evaded the draft, of whom 200,000 were indicted for draft offenses; 300,000 people sought conscientious objector (CO) deferments and were denied; another 170,000 received CO status; between 30,000 and 50,000 left the U.S. for Canada and another 20,000 or so sought refuge underground in the U.S. or abroad. Until 1967, only those who could claim and prove specific religious prohibitions against participating in a war received CO status. But various court rulings broadened the grounds on which

Antiwar protesters in Washington, D.C., October 1967. The number and size of demonstrations increased as the war escalated; this demonstration attracted more than 100,000 people and included acts of civil disobedience. After a night's vigil, demonstrators were violently dispersed by troops with bayonets.

I-Feel-Like-I'm-Fixin'-to-Die Rag

Opinions on serving in Vietnam were often reflected in the lyrics of popular songs of the period. "I-Feel-Like-I'm-Fixin'-to-Die Rag" by Country Joe and the Fish was first heard in Berkeley, California, in 1965 and was a big hit at New York's Woodstock Music and Art Fair in 1969. It circulated widely among servicemen in Vietnam and was played on personal tapes in the field.

Come on all you big strong men,
Uncle Sam needs your help again;
He's got himself in a terrible jam
way down yonder in Vietnam;
So put down your books and pick up a gun,
We're gonna have a whole lot of fun.

Chorus:
And it's 1, 2, 3. What are we fighting for?
Don't ask me, I don't give a damn.
Next stop is Vietnam.
And it's 5, 6, 7. Open up the Pearly Gates;
There ain't no time to wonder why,

Whoopie—we're all gonna die.
Come on generals, let's move fast,
Your big chance has come at last;
Now you can go out and get those Reds,
The only good Commie is one that's dead;
You know that peace can only be won,
When we've blown 'em all to Kingdom come!

Chorus

Come on, Wall Street, don't move slow,
Why, man, this is war Au-go-go;
There's plenty good money to be made,
Supplying the army with tools of the trade;
Don't be afraid they'll drop The Bomb.
They'll drop it on the Viet Cong!

Chorus

Well come on mothers throughout the land,
Pack your boys off to Vietnam.
Come on fathers don't hesitate,
Send them off before it's too late.
Be the first one on your block,
To have your boy come home in a box.

The antiwar movement made a special effort to appeal to African Americans, for whom military service was often a way out of poverty.

one could seek a CO deferment. As a result, many men who held strong moral beliefs that barred participation in the military, but were not necessarily members of a peace church or did not hold a specific belief in a Supreme Being who they understood as prohibiting war, were now eligible. Moreover, some 17,000 applications came from men already serving in the military, who for a variety of reasons felt they could not, in good conscience, complete their tour of duty.

The draft resistance movement involved some surprising figures. Muhammad Ali, the heavyweight boxing champion, was one. On April 28, 1967, Ali refused induction into the armed forces on the grounds that he was a minister in the Nation of Islam, an African-American Islamic group. Retribution was swift: within an hour of his refusal, the New York State Athletic Commission suspended his boxing license and other state commissions followed suit. His subsequent trial for refusing induction resulted in a five-year prison sentence

and a $10,000 fine, both of which were reversed on appeal.
Below is Ali's reflection on his decision not to serve.

I never thought of myself as great when I refused to go into the Army. All I did was stand up for what I believed. There were people who thought the war in Vietnam was right. And those people, if they went to war, acted just as brave as I did. There were people who tried to put me in jail. Some of them were hypocrites, but others did what they thought was proper and I can't condemn them for following their conscience either. People say I made a sacrifice, risking jail and my whole career. But God told Abraham to kill his son and Abraham was willing to do it, so why shouldn't I follow what I believed? Standing up for my religion made me happy; it wasn't a sacrifice. When people got drafted and sent to Vietnam and didn't understand what the killing was about and came home with one leg and couldn't get jobs, that was a sacrifice. But I believed in what I was doing, so no matter what the government did to me, it wasn't a loss.

Some people thought I was a hero. Some people said that what I did was wrong. But everything I did was according to my conscience. I wasn't trying to be a leader. I just wanted to be free. And I made a stand all people, not just black people, should have thought about making, because it wasn't just black people being drafted. The government had a system where the rich man's son went to college, and the poor man's son went to war. Then, after the rich man's son got out of college, he did other things to keep him out of the Army until he was too old to be drafted. So what I did was for me, but it was the kind of decision everyone has to make. Freedom, means being able to follow your religion, but it also means carrying the responsibility to choose between right and wrong. So when the time came for me to make up my mind about going in the Army, I knew people were dying in Vietnam for nothing and I should live by what I thought was right. I wanted America to be America. And now the whole world knows that, so far as my own beliefs are concerned, I did what was right for me.

The most revered civil rights leader in the country, Martin Luther King Jr., first spoke out against the war in July, 1965, in a speech urging negotiations. The National Association for the Advancement of Colored People (NAACP) was sharply critical of the speech, less on grounds of principle than tactics, given Johnson's efforts on behalf of civil rights legislation. For a time, King avoided commenting on the war but in

The Fighting Side of Me

Merle Haggard offered his views on the war in his song "The Fighting Side of Me." As opposed to the songs heard on the tape players of soldiers in the fields, Haggard's songs were played on the official Armed Forces radio station.

I hear people talking bad about the way
they have to live here in this country.
Harping on the wars they fight and
griping about the ways things ought to be.

I don't mind them switching sides and
standing up for things they believe in.
When they're running down our country, man,
they are walking on the fighting side of me.

Chorus:
They're walking on the fighting side of me.
Running down our way of life our fighting men
have fought and died to keep.

If you don't love it—leave it,
let this song that I am singing be a warning.
When you are running down our country, hoss,
then you are walking on the fighting side of me.

I read about some squirrely guy who claims
that he just don't believe in fighting
and I wonder just how long the rest of us
can count on being free.

They love our milk and honey,
but they preach about some other way of living.
When they are running down our country,
man, they're walking on the fighting side of me.

Chorus

The racial tensions of the 1960s did not disappear with the war. This banner, carried by antiwar demonstrators (some of them veterans), expressed the sentiment of many African Americans who continued to suffer discrimination at home while being asked to risk their lives abroad fighting a nonwhite enemy.

late 1966, increasingly distressed by the escalation of the war and the spreading violence in major American cities, he joined Clergy and Laity Concerned About Vietnam (CALCAV). In March 1967 King led an antiwar demonstration in Chicago and then on April 4, 1967, he delivered a major address at Riverside Church in New York in which he openly attacked the administration's war policies.

I come to this magnificent House of Worship tonight because my conscience leaves me no other choice. . . . [I agree with the sentiment] "A time comes when silence is betrayal." That time has come for us in relation to Vietnam . . . men do not easily assume the task of opposing their government, especially in time of war . . . .

Over the past two years, as I have moved to break the betrayal of my own silences and to speak from the burnings of my own heart, as I have called for radical departures from the destruction of Vietnam, many persons have questioned me about the wisdom of my path. . . . Peace and civil rights don't mix, they say. . . .

I come to this platform tonight to make a passionate plea to my beloved nation. This speech is not addressed to Hanoi or to the

National Liberation Front. It is not addressed to China or to Russia. . . . Tonight . . . I wish . . . to speak . . . to my fellow Americans who, with me, bear the greatest responsibility in ending a conflict that has exacted a heavy price on both continents. . . .

A few years ago . . . there was a real promise of hope for the poor—both black and white—through the poverty program. . . . Then came the buildup in Vietnam and I watched the program broken and eviscerated. . . . I knew that America would never invest the necessary funds or energies in rehabilitation of its poor so long as adventures like Vietnam continued to draw men and skills and money like some demonic destructive suction tube. So I was increasingly compelled to see the war as an enemy of the poor. . . .

It became clear to me that the war was doing far more than devastating the hopes of the poor at home. It was sending their sons and their brothers and their husbands to fight and to die in extraordinarily high proportions relative to the rest of the population. We were taking the black young men who had been crippled by our society and sending them eight thousand miles away to guarantee liberties in Southeast Asia which they had not found in southwest Georgia and East Harlem. . . .

[My opposition] . . . grows out of my experience in the ghettos of the North over the last three years. . . . As I have walked among the desperate, rejected and angry young men I have told them that Molotov cocktails and rifles would not solve their problems. . . . But they asked—and rightly so—what about Vietnam? They asked if our own nation wasn't using massive doses of

Sergeant Donald Duncan was a 10-year veteran and one of the earliest recruits to the Special Forces. In March 1965, he refused a field promotion to the rank of captain, and in September he received his honorable discharge papers. Duncan recalls his thoughts on the the incident in this excerpt from an article in Ramparts *magazine.*

But were we stopping communism?. . . The more troops and money we poured in, the more people hated us. . . .

The whole thing was a lie. We weren't preserving freedom in South Vietnam. There was no freedom to preserve. To voice opposition to the government meant jail or death.

Martin Luther King Jr. speaking at Girard College, Philadelphia, in 1965. King's classic oratorical style inspired both the civil rights and the antiwar movement. He was assassinated in 1968.

violence to solve its problems, to bring about the changes it wanted. Their questions hit home, and I knew that I could never again raise my voice against the violence of the oppressed in the ghettos without having first spoken clearly to the greatest purveyor of violence in the world today—my own government. . . .

As I ponder the madness of Vietnam and search within myself for ways to understand and respond with compassion my mind goes constantly to the people of that peninsula . . . it is clear to me that there will be no meaningful solution there until some attempt is made to know them and hear their broken cries. . . .

They watch as we poison their water, as we kill a million acres of their crops. They must weep as the bulldozers roar through their areas preparing to destroy the precious trees. They wander into the hospitals, with at least twenty casualties from American firepower for one "Viet Cong"–inflicted injury. So far we may have killed a million of them—mostly children. . . .

We have destroyed their two most cherished institutions: the family and the village. We have destroyed their land and their crops. . . . We have corrupted their women and children and killed their men. What liberators! . . .

Somehow this madness must cease. We must stop now. I speak as a child of God and brother to the suffering poor of Vietnam. . . . I speak for the poor of America who are paying the double price of smashed hopes at home and death and corruption in Vietnam. . . .

In order to atone for our sins and errors in Vietnam, we should take the initiative in bringing a halt to this tragic war . . .

1. *End all bombing* . . .
2. *Declare a unilateral cease-fire* . . .
3. *Take immediate steps to prevent other battlefields in Southeast Asia* . . .
4. *Realistically accept the . . . National Liberation Front has substantial support in South Vietnam*
5. *Set a date that we will remove all foreign troops from Vietnam* . . .

Meanwhile we in the churches and synagogues have a continuing task while we urge our government to disengage itself from a disgraceful commitment. We must continue to raise our voices . . . We must be prepared to match actions with words by seeking out every creative means of protest possible.

As we counsel young men concerning military service we must clarify for them our nation's role in Vietnam and challenge them with the alternative of conscientious objection. . . . Moreover I would encourage all ministers of draft age to give up their ministerial exemptions and seek status as conscientious objectors. . . .

We must move past indecision to action. We must find new ways to speak for peace in Vietnam and justice throughout the developing world. . . .

Malcolm X was a prominent African-American activist whose fiery rhetoric attracted an increasing number of adherents to the separatist Nation of Islam (Black Muslims). In 1964 he split with that organization, arguing for a secular and potentially more inclusive version of black nationalism. He was assassinated on February 21, 1965; three members of the Black Muslims were tried and convicted for the crime, though skepticism remains as to who was actually responsible. In the course of a speech to the Militant Labor Forum in New York City on January 7, 1965, Malcom X said he wanted to talk about Vietnam "for two minutes":

It's a shame—that's one second. It is, it's a shame. You put the government on the spot when you even mention Vietnam. They feel embarrassed—you notice that? They wish they would not even have to read the newspapers about South Vietnam, and you can't blame them. It's just a trap that they let themselves get into. It's John Foster Dulles they're trying to blame it on, because he's dead.

But they're trapped, they can't get out. You notice I said "they." They are trapped, they can't get out. If they pour more men in, they'll get deeper. If they pull the men out, it's a defeat. And they should have known it in the first place.

France had about 200,000 Frenchmen over there, and the most highly mechanized modern army sitting on this earth. And those little rice farmers ate them up, and their tanks, and everything else. Yes, they did, and France was deeply entrenched, had been there for a hundred or more years. Now, if she couldn't stay there and was entrenched, why, you are out of your mind if you think Sam can get in over there.

But we're not supposed to say that. If we say that, we're anti-American, or we're

A poster of Malcolm X denouncing the war as "criminal." This poster shows Malcolm with his arm extended in appeal and argument, but most news photographs of Malcolm depicted him in more threatening oratorical poses.

What America is doing in South Vietnam is criminal... We see where the problem of Vietnam is the problem of the oppressed and the oppressor...Our action will be one of unity and in the unity of oppressed people is actually the strength, and the best strength of the oppressed people....

THIRD WORLD PEOPLE UNITE AGAINST THE WAR

Third World Committee—SMC—15 East 17th St., N.Y., N.Y., 10003 (212) 675-8465

seditious, or we're subversive, or we're advocating something that's not intelligent. So that's two minutes, sir.

Opposition within the Military

In 1967 six Vietnam veterans formed an organization whose name embodied their purpose: Vietnam Veterans Against the War (VVAW). They reasoned that if any American had the right to speak out against the war, it was the men who had been called upon to fight in it. By 1970 VVAW had 600 members and it grew exponentially over the next few years. In January 1971 VVAW held three days of public testimony at a motel in Detroit during which some 100 veterans testified to the crimes of war they had either witnessed or in which they had participated.

From April 19 to April 23, 1971, VVAW also led demonstrations in Washington. Leaders called their protest "a limited incursion into the country of Congress," and named it Dewey Canyon III (on the model of Dewey Canyon I and Dewey Canyon II, code names for American and then ARVN invasions of Laos in February and March 1971). The VVAW set up an encampment in Potomac Park, marched with the mothers of soldiers who had died in Vietnam to Arlington National Cemetery, gave street theater performances, lobbied Congress, and, in dramatic culmination, 700 veterans tried to return their medals and ribbons to Congress. The response of the Nixon administration was to order a court injunction against the encampment and erect a wooden barrier around the Capitol building, over which the veterans threw their medals, stating their names and the nature of the decorations as they did so. John Kerry, a decorated combat veteran, former Navy lieutenant (and later, Democratic Senator from Massachusetts) testified before the Senate Foreign Relations Committee.

The Dewey Canyon III demonstration by Vietnam Veterans Against the War was titled after the code name for the invasions of Laos. Rusty Sachs, one of the organizers, returns his medal in the name of friends who have died in Vietnam. Barriers in front of the Capitol building had been erected to "protect" Congress from the invading veterans.

Thank you very much, Senator Fulbright, Senator Javits, Senator Symington, Senator Pell. I would like to say for the record, and also for the men behind me who are also wearing the uniform and their medals, that my sitting here is really symbolic. I am not here as John Kerry. I am here as one member of the group of 1,000 which is a small representation of a very much larger group of veterans in this country, and were it possible for all of them to sit at this table they would be here and have the same kind of testimony.

I would simply like to speak in very general terms. . . . several months ago in Detroit we had an investigation at which over 150 honorably discharged, and many very highly decorated, veterans testified to war crimes committed in Southeast Asia. These were not isolated incidents but crimes committed on a day to day basis with the full awareness of officers at all levels of command. It is impossible to describe to you exactly what did happen in Detroit—the emotions in the room and the feelings of the men who were reliving their experiences in Vietnam. They relived the absolute horror of what this country, in a sense, made them do.

They told stories that at times they had personally raped, cut off ears, cut off heads, taped wires from portable telephones to human genitals and turned up the power, cut off limbs, blown up bodies, randomly shot at civilians, razed villages in fashion reminiscent of Genghis Khan, shot cattle and dogs for fun, poisoned food stocks, and generally ravaged the countryside of South Vietnam in addition to the normal ravage of war and the normal and very particular ravaging which is done by the applied bombing power of this country. We call this investigation the Winter Soldier Investigation. The term Winter Soldier is a play on words of Thomas Paine's in 1776 when he spoke of the Sunshine Patriots and summertime soldiers who deserted at Valley Forge because the going was rough.

We who have come here to Washington have come here because we feel we have to be winter soldiers now. . . . The country doesn't know it yet but it has created a monster, a monster in the form of millions of men who have been taught to deal and to trade in violence and who are given the chance to die for the biggest nothing in history; men who have returned with a sense of anger and a sense of betrayal which no one has yet grasped. . . . We are angry because we feel we have been used in the worst fashion by the administration of this country.

In 1970 at West Point Vice President Agnew said, "Some glamorize the criminal misfits of society while our best men die in Asian rice paddies to preserve the freedom which most of those misfits abuse," and this was used as a rallying point for our effort in Vietnam.

But for us, as boys in Asia whom the country was supposed to support, his statement is a terrible distortion from which we can only draw a very deep sense of revulsion, and hence the anger of

A Look Back

Colonel David H. Hackworth is a veteran of World War II, Korea, and Vietnam, and one of the most highly decorated soldiers in U.S. military history. In an interview, excerpted below, Hackworth expresses his feelings about the Vietnam War.

Not a day passes without my seeing the faces of the men who died under my command during my five tours of duty in Vietnam. . . . They were all young, just boys who couldn't buy a beer in their hometowns. But they were deemed old enough by politicians to kill and be killed. . . . They believed in me, and I believed in our country, our cause and our mission.

I discovered too late that the enemy was motivated not by ideology but by freedom and independence. It was only then that I realized we had no business being there . . . But in Vietnam I discovered that most of the senior leadership was concerned mainly with themselves and neither understood the nature of the war nor had a clue about the impossible mission with which they'd tasked their soldiers. . . .

I told the press that Americans were being lied to, that the war was unwinnable the way it was being fought, and that we should get the hell out. . . .

I was in Vietnam from 1965 through 1971, down in the field where the dying occurred . . . . each year our efforts became weaker while our "snuffed out" opponents

The Vietnam Reality

On Veterans Day, November 11, 1967, Joseph A. Scerra, commander in chief of the Veterans of Foreign Wars of the United States, spoke at ceremonies held in Birmingham, Alabama. His speech was entitled "The Vietnam Reality."

We—through retrospect—may even wish that we had not become involved in South Viet-Nam. We may even harbor the vain idea that our mission in South Viet-Nam was not necessary—but regardless of this looking back—we are faced with the reality of today. Three Presidents—and the sessions of our elected representatives in Congress . . . decided that it was in the interest of this nation—in the interest of freedom—in the interest of world peace—that we DO become involved in that nation. We now honor our commitment. . . .

A nation intent upon its own way of life was invaded by another nation. . . . And—in strict obedience to our conscience and the American principles of liberty for all men— we came to their rescue. . . .

It seems to me that for a long time Americans have thought about the war as if they were watching a television program. That the bloodshed, and the reason Americans were fighting was somebody else's war—that it was a panorama, that we could get rid of by switching off the set. . . . So, in reality, we owe those who dissented a debt of gratitude. They have brought us to our senses—they brought the fact right to our doorsteps—to the sanctity of our living rooms. We realized that the battle was not in Viet-Nam alone— for it was erupting within our own nation. Because of this, we have united.

some of the men who are here in Washington today. It is a distortion because we in no way consider ourselves the best men of this country; because those he calls misfits were standing up for us in a way that nobody else in this country dared to; because so many who have died would have returned to this country to join the misfits in their efforts to ask for an immediate withdrawal from South Vietnam; because so many of those best men have returned as quadriplegics and amputees—and they lie forgotten in Veterans Administration Hospitals in this country which fly the flag which so many have chosen as their own personal symbol—and we cannot consider ourselves America's best men when we are ashamed of and hated for what we were called on to do in Southeast Asia.

In our opinion, and from our experience, there is nothing in South Vietnam which could happen that realistically threatens the United States of America. . . .

I know that all of you talk about every possible alternative for getting out of Vietnam. We understand that. We know you have considered the seriousness of the aspects to the utmost level and I am not going to try to dwell on that. But I want to relate to you the feeling that many of the men who have returned to this country express because we are probably angriest about all that we were told about Vietnam and about the mystical war against communism.

We found that not only was it a civil war, an effort by a people who had for years been seeking their liberation from any colonial influence whatsoever, but also we found that the Vietnamese whom we had enthusiastically molded after our own image were hard put to take up the fight against the threat we were supposedly saving them from.

We saw Vietnam ravaged equally by American bombs and search and destroy missions, as well as by Viet Cong terrorism, and yet we listened while this country tried to blame all of the havoc on the Viet Cong.

We rationalized destroying villages in order to save them. We saw America lose her sense of morality as she accepted very coolly a My Lai and refused to give up the image of American soldiers who hand out chocolate bars and chewing gum.

We learned the meaning of free fire zones, shooting anything that moves, and we watched while America placed a cheapness on the lives of Orientals. We watched the United States falsification of body counts, in fact the glorification of body counts. We listened while month after month we were told the back of the enemy was about to break. . . .

We are asking here in Washington for some action; action from the Congress of the United States of America which has the power to raise and maintain armies, and which by the Constitution also has the power to declare war. We have come here, not to the President, because we believe that this body can be responsive to the will of the people, and we believe that the will of the people says that we should be out of Vietnam now. . . .

Finally this administration has done us the ultimate dishonor. They have attempted to disown us and the sacrifices we made for this country. In their blindness and fear they have tried to deny that we are veterans or that we served in Nam. We do not need their testimony. Our own scars and stumps of limbs are witness enough for others and for ourselves.

New York mounted police separated pro-war from antiwar demonstrators, though scuffles and name-calling between the two groups were frequent at all demonstrations.

Chapter 7

Nixon's War

Richard Milhous Nixon assumed the Presidency on January 20, 1969, with an overwhelming mandate from the American people: to make peace in Vietnam. He claimed to have a "secret plan" to end the war, but it quickly became apparent that it was a plan to continue the war by other means.

Nixon's first effort was to pull the teeth of the antiwar movement. He countered evidence that antiwar sentiment (of varying intensity) expressed the majority sentiment on the war, by appealing to what he called the "silent majority." This tactic shifted the focus of debate from the goals of the antiwar protesters to the manner in which they protested. Second, he reduced the volume of American casualties by withdrawing American troops (confining the American effort to the air), increasing artillery and aerial bombardment, and leaving ground operations to the South Vietnamese, a policy he called "Vietnamization." American air power centered on saturation B-52 bomber raids over North Vietnam. Nixon reasoned that much of the opposition to the war stemmed from the inequities of the draft. In 1969 he instituted a lottery system based on one's date of birth in which everyone took their chances equally. In 1973 he eliminated conscription completely in favor of an all-volunteer military.

Although he was convinced that only a sharp escalation of the war would force the National Liberation Front to make peace on terms that would preserve a separate anticommunist regime in the South, Nixon continued the public peace talks in Paris begun at the end of the Johnson administration. To these he added high-level secrets talks conducted by Henry Kissinger, who served first as national security advisor and later as secretary of state. One focus of the talks was the demand for the immediate release of American prisoners of war, an instantly comprehensible and popular goal. The North Vietnamese, for their part, insisted that a cease-fire agreement must accompany any discussion of prisoner exchange. The Nixon administration presented this

Early in his Presidency, Nixon went to Vietnam in order to boost the troops' morale as well as his own.

An angry pro-war demonstrator makes his feelings clear in his lapel buttons: "Better Dead than Red," one declares; the other is a militaristic version of the peace symbol—a bomber is used instead of the standard lines.

stalemate to the public as evidence that the war continued solely because Hanoi refused to release American prisoners.

Meanwhile, earlier rationales for the war began to lose force. Starting with the Eisenhower administration, the U.S. had always claimed that Chinese Communist power would be enhanced—and American security threatened—by a North Vietnamese victory. One war aim, therefore, had been to control and contain Communist China. Then, in 1971, to the surprise of virtually the entire world, Nixon moved toward reconciliation with Communist China. And in 1972 both Nixon and Kissinger traveled to China hoping its leaders would be able to persuade North Vietnam to settle the war on terms acceptable to the United States. The Chinese were pleased to move towards normal relations with the United States but did little to help extricate the Nixon administration from the war.

Working at diplomatic, military, and public relations levels simultaneously, Nixon kept to a steady schedule of troop withdrawal and "Vietnamization." The tactical goal was to wipe out North Vietnamese supply bases and sanctuaries in Cambodia and Laos. To this end, Cambodia was invaded in 1970 in a joint U.S.—South Vietnamese operation; the South Vietnamese conducted their own operation in Laos in 1971 and saturation bombing by B-52s was dramatically stepped up over North Vietnam, Cambodia, and Laos.

Opposition to the war continued, most particularly in Congress, as the politicians began to feel the growing public anger. Now Congress sought to limit Nixon's power to expand the war. Throughout this period, "secret" peace talks in Paris continued and finally, after compromises on both sides, a cease-fire agreement between the United States and the Democratic Republic of Vietnam seemed to have been reached in October 1972. One major problem remained: how to get the South Vietnamese government, which was party to the talks, to agree. As long as the United States stayed engaged in the war, the South Vietnamese could not lose, though they might not be able to win, either.

The peace agreement would end American military participation, leaving the contesting parties to work toward a political solution to the long civil war. Nguyen Van Thieu, president of South Vietnam since 1967, had reason to believe he could not win politically and threatened to reject the agreement. In order to reassure him that the United States stood ready to reengage (in terms of air power and aid) if need be, Nixon ordered a last, massive bombing raid of Hanoi and the port city Haiphong, from December 18–29, 1972, usually referred to as the "Christmas Bombing." In January 1973, the cease-fire agreement was finally signed on terms virtually identical to those available before the bombing. The Vietnam war became, at last, a war among the Vietnamese. Any possibility of American reengagement ended with the Watergate scandal and the subsequent impeachment hearings that led to Nixon's resignation. On April 30, 1975, the 30-year war ended in a decisive victory for Hanoi and the National Liberation Front.

My Lai

The first Vietnam crisis of Nixon's administration had actually occurred a year before he took office. In March 1968, Charlie Company of the Americal Division's 11th Infantry Brigade massacred virtually the entire population of My Lai hamlet. No shots were fired other than by Americans and there were no American casualties, although more than 400 Vietnamese were killed, mainly women and children. The incident was covered up at the time, but was revealed through the efforts of Vietnam veteran Ron L. Ridenhour. Ultimately, Congressman Morris Udall of Arizona raised questions that could not be avoided.

The Army ordered a special investigation of My Lai, headed by Lieutenant General William Peers, which charged 224 violations of the military code. Charges were filed against a number of senior officers, some of whom were later demoted for the cover-up. Only one man was convicted: Lieutenant William Calley was sentenced to life imprisonment for the premeditated murder of 22 civilians. According to the Nixon White House, telegrams ran 100 to 1 in favor of clemency. Nixon released Calley, pending his appeal; in 1974 the sentence was reduced to 10 years, with parole possible at the end of the year. Shortly after Nixon's resignation in 1974, Calley was paroled.

What follows is an eyewitness account of the events in the village that fateful day. Warrant Officer Hugh Thompson Jr. had landed his helicopter in the midst of the massacre in order to rescue wounded Vietnamese. The day after My Lai, Thompson had informed a senior officer, Colonel Oran K. Henderson, about what had happened. Henderson took no action. In March 1998, the army finally recognized Thompson and his crew by awarding them the Soldier's Medal for gallantry.

Madman Theory

Strolling on the beach with aide H. R. (Bob) Haldeman during the 1968 presidential campaign, Nixon confided his strategy for victory in Vietnam:

I'm the one man in this country who can do it. They'll believe any threat of force that Nixon makes because it's Nixon. I call it the Madman Theory, Bob. I want the North Vietnamese to believe I've reached the point where I might do anything to stop the war. We'll just slip the word to them that, "for God's sake, you know Nixon is obsessed about Communism. We can't restrain him when he's angry and he has his hand on the nuclear button" and Ho Chi Minh himself will be in Paris in two days begging for peace.

When I saw the bodies in the ditch I came back around and saw that some of them were still alive. So I sat [the helicopter] down on the ground and then talked to—I'm pretty sure it was a sergeant . . . and I told them that there was women and kids over there that were wounded—could he help them or could they help them? And he made some remark to the effect that the only way he could help them was to kill them and I thought he was joking. I didn't take him seriously . . . and I took off again. And as I took off my crew chief said that the guy was shooting into the ditch . . . .

I saw this bunker and either the crew chief or the gunner said that there was a bunch of kids in the bunker, and the Americans were approaching it. . . . so I set down . . . got out of the aircraft and talked with this lieutenant, and told him that there was some women and kids in that bunker over there, and could he get them out. He said the only way to get them out was with a hand grenade. I told him to just hold your men right where they are and I'll get the kids out. And I walked over towards the bunker, motioned for them to come out, and they came out. [There were too many for Thompson to take on board.] . . . and I called Mr. Millians who was flying the low gun cover and told him what I had and asked him if he'd come in and get them out of this immediate area . . . and he came in and picked up half of them.

Thompson was not the only one who spoke out about what he saw at My Lai. The testimony below comes from Dennis Conti, one of several members of Charlie Company who refused to follow Calley's orders to "take care of them."

They were bringing people out, and then we pushed them out into the rice paddy, onto the dike there. And, like I said, we pushed them out of there. . . . Meadlo and myself, we watched them. . . . There were a woman and a baby about 4 years old, who were walking, and an older woman, who I assumed to be a grandmother or something. I rounded them up, brought them back down to Meadlo, and we stood around them for a couple of minutes talking. Lieutenant Calley came back, and said: "Take care of them," So we said: "Okay." And we sat there and watched them like we usually do. And he came back again, and he said: "I thought I told you to take care of them." I said: "We're taking care of them." and he said: "I mean kill them." So I looked at Meadlo, and he looked at me, and I didn't want to do it, and he didn't want to do it . . . then [Calley] said: "Come on, we'll line them up here, we'll kill them." So I told him: "I'll watch the tree line." . . . I had

NIXON'S BOMBS KILL PEOPLE

the M-79, I figured that was a good excuse. . . . [Calley then gave the order to fire.] Then they opened up, and started firing. Meadlo fired a while. I don't know how much he fired, a clip, I think. It might have been more. He started to cry, and he gave me his weapon. I took it and he told me to kill them. And I said I wasn't going to kill them. At the time, when we were talking, the only thing left was children. I told Meadlo, I said: "I'm not going to kill them. [Calley] looks like he's enjoying it. I'm going to let him do it." So, like I said, the only thing left was children. He [Calley] started killing the children.

Seymour Hersh was the first journalist to take the My Lai story seriously. Two major American magazines, *Life* and *Look*, refused to buy the story. Eventually he sold it to the Dispatch News Service, an independent, antiwar news agency. Dispatch News then offered the story to 52 newspapers and magazines; thirty-six of them agreed to it. One army officer expressed amazement that it had taken the press so long to hear about the incident. These are excerpts from the series Hersh wrote.

These factors are not in dispute:

The . . . area . . . had been a Viet Cong fortress since the Vietnam war began. In early February 1968, a company of the Eleventh Brigade, as part of Task Force Barker, pushed through the area and was severely shot up.

The area was a free fire zone from which all non-Viet Cong residents had been urged, by leaflet, to flee. Such zones are common throughout Vietnam.

Artist Paul Conrad responded to the story that Americans were more upset by the publicity about the My Lai massacre than the massacre itself. In this cartoon, he illustrates willful blindness to the event.

Newsweek Poll on My Lai

Do you approve or disapprove of the court-martial finding that Lieutenant Calley is guilty of premeditated murder?

Approve 9%
Disapprove 79%
No opinion 12%

If you disapprove, do you disapprove of the verdict because you think that what happened at My Lai was not a crime, or because you think many others besides Calley share responsibility for what happened?

Not a crime 20%
Others responsible . . 71%
Both 1%
Other 7%
No response 1%

Do you think Lieutenant Calley is being made the scapegoat for the actions of others above him, or not?

Yes 69%
No 12%
No opinion 19%

Do you think the incident for which Lieutenant Calley was tried was an isolated incident or a common one?

Isolated 24%
Common 50%
No opinion 26%

Do you approve or disapprove of President Nixon's decision to release Lieutenant Calley pending appeal of his conviction?

Approve 83%
Disapprove 7%
No opinion 10%

Some people have suggested that the U.S. is guilty of war crimes in Vietnam for which high government and military officials should be tried. Do you agree or disagree?

Agree 32%
Disagree 47%
No opinion 21%

Poll reports more Americans disturbed over My Lai publicity than My Lai massacre itself.

One man who took part in the mission with Calley said that in the earlier two attacks, "we were really shot up."

"Every time we got hit it was from the rear," he said. "So the third time in there the order came down to go in and make sure no one was behind. We were told to just clear the area. It was a typical combat assault formation. We came in hot, with a cover of artillery in front of us, came down the line and destroyed the village. There are always some civilian casualties in a combat operation. He [Calley] isn't guilty of murder." . . .

Calley's friends in the officer corps at Fort Benning, many of them West Point graduates, are indignant. . . . "They're using this as a Goddamned example," one officer complained. "He's a good soldier. He followed orders. There weren't any friendlies in the village. The orders were to shoot anything that moved."

Another officer said, "It could happen to any of us. He has killed and has seen a lot of killing. . . . Killing becomes nothing in Vietnam. He knew there were civilians there, but he also knew that there were VC among them."

A third officer . . . said: "There's this question—I think anyone who goes to Nam asks it. What's a civilian? Someone who works for us at day and puts on Viet Cong pajamas at night?" . . . One Pentagon officer discussing the case tapped his knee with his hand and remarked, "Some of those kids he shot were this high. I don't think they were Viet Cong. Do you?"

[Sgt. Michael] Bernhardt said that about 90% of the 60 to 70 men in the short-handed company were involved in the shootings. He took no part, he said. "I only shoot at people who shoot at me," was his explanation.

"The Army ordered me not to talk," Bernhardt told the interviewer. "But there are some orders that I have to personally decide whether to obey; I have my own conscience to consider." . . .

Why did it happen?

"I think that probably the officers didn't really know if they were ordered to kill the villagers or not. . . . A lot of guys feel that they (the South Vietnamese civilians) aren't human beings; we just treated them like animals."

"We were under orders," Meadlo said. "We all thought we were doing the right thing. . . . At the time it didn't bother me."

He began having serious doubts that night about what he had done. . . . He says he still has them. . . .

"In the beginning," Meadlo said, "I just thought we were going to be murdering the Viet Cong. . . . They didn't put up a fight or anything. The women huddled against their children and took it. They brought their kids real close to their stomachs and hugged them, and put their bodies over them trying to save them. It didn't do much good," Meadlo said.

The conservative periodical *National Review* defended the American mission in Vietnam in a piece written before Lieutenant Calley's court-martial.

Whether atrocities were committed at [My Lai] we do not as yet know; but more than enough atrocities against human reason have been committed in response by the American media. "That America and Americans must stand in the larger dock of guilt and human conscience for what happened at My Lai seems inescapable." So observed *Time*, adding: "Men in American uniforms slaughtered the civilians of My Lai, and in so doing humiliated the U.S. and called in question the U.S. mission in Vietnam in a way that all the antiwar protesters could never have done." One's mind staggers: Are "America and Americans" generally guilty? . . . And

The poster of Calley below, with the dictionary definition of the word "scapegoat," illustrates what many people, both pro- and antiwar, felt about his trial. Those who supported the war believed Calley had done only what was necessary; those who opposed it believed Calley's superiors should have been in the dock with him.

Painful Memories

Ha Thi Quy, a woman who survived the My Lai massacre, remembered the day in an interview.

In the early morning, just after we got up, the helicopters came and started shelling, and soldiers poured out onto the fields. I was eating breakfast. We thought it might be like the other times the Americans came into the village. They gave the children candy. Or like the second time, when Americans came to take water from the well to fill their canteens, and then left, and they didn't do any harm to the people. But the third time, March 16, 1968, when they came to the hamlet they rounded up all the people. Some they took to the roadside and shot right away. . . . And some they brought over to this ditch, here. First they shot Mr. Cau. He was a monk. He lived in the pagoda. Then they forced everyone into the ditch and shot them. I was wounded in the backside. . . . And they killed—you see, they fired a first time into the ditch, and many men, children and women were killed. They cried "Mother." They were screaming. . . .

Afterwards, I got up to go back to my house, and I saw nothing. All the houses had been burned. They had cut down our village tree by the pond. They had cut all the trees down in the orchards. They had killed everyone. There were dead bodies all over the village. I took a little dead baby back to the house from the roadside. It was my daughter's child.

I went to the next hamlet and found my younger sister-in-law killed, lying on the floor. And I found her daughter's body, a fifteen-year-old girl, all her clothing torn off and her legs were spread open—raped by the Americans.

They had no mercy, the Americans. You see, they had come here many times and we got along with them. Then they came and killed all the people. . . . We had done nothing to them. . . . Twice before, the Americans had come here and done nothing. We don't understand why the third time they killed the people.

even if it turns out that atrocities were committed, how does this call in question the U.S. mission in Vietnam? Do the innumerable atrocities committed by both sides in World War II add up to the proposition that resistance to the Nazis ought to have been abandoned? On April 9–10, 1948, Israeli commandos massacred all 254 inhabitants of the Arab village of Deir Yassin—men, women, and children. Does *Time* conclude from this that the Israeli position, in toto, is morally indefensible? During the American Civil War atrocity was not an aberration, the act of bewildered or temporarily unbalanced men, but a matter of settled military policy. "Until we can repopulate Georgia," said General Sherman, "it is useless for us to occupy it; but the utter destruction of its roads, houses, and people will cripple their military resources." Does *Time* conclude that the Union, therefore, should have been permitted to disintegrate? Irrational and irresponsible comment on [My Lai] has become collective madness.

The Nixon Doctrine

In a speech on November 3, 1969, President Nixon outlined his future policy. He committed the country to the pursuit of victory in Vietnam, rejecting total withdrawal of U.S. troops but promising to shift the burden of ground combat to the South Vietnamese themselves. This would allow phased withdrawal of American troops and thus a likely decrease in antiwar protests. In addition, the United States would continue the air war as well as military and financial aid to South Vietnam. Finally, Nixon placed the onus of the war on the North Vietnamese who, he claimed, refused to accept his peace proposals.

Nixon insisted that North Vietnamese and American troops in Vietnam were equally "outside forces." The North Vietnamese, on the other hand, refused to acknowledge they had any troops at all in the South, their way of insisting that the only "foreign" troops in the country were American. In his memoirs, Nixon described the origins of his first major address to the country on the war.

I knew that the opponents of the war would irrevocably become my opponents if my speech took a hard line. But I could not escape the fact that I felt it would be wrong to end the Vietnam war on any terms I believed to be less than honorable.

I worked through the night. About 4 A.M. I wrote a paragraph calling for the support of "the great silent majority of Americans." I went to bed, but after two hours of restless sleep I was wide awake, so I got up and began work again. By 8 A.M. the speech was finished. I called Haldeman, and when he answered, I said, "The baby's just been born!"

The message of my November 3 speech was that we were going to keep our commitment in Vietnam. We were going to continue fighting until the Communists agreed to negotiate a fair and honorable peace or until the South Vietnamese were able to defend themselves on their own—whichever came first. At the same time we would continue our disengagement based on the principles of the Nixon Doctrine: the pace of withdrawal would be linked to the progress of Vietnamization, the level of enemy activity, and developments on the negotiating front. I emphasized that our policy would not be affected by demonstrations in the streets.

At least in part because of the very different expectations that had been built up around this speech, my strongly expressed determination to stand and fight came as a surprise to many people and therefore had a greatly increased impact. I called on the American people for their support:

I have chosen a plan for peace. I believe it will succeed. If it does succeed, what the critics say now won't matter. If it does not succeed, anything I say then won't matter. . . .

And so tonight—to you, the great silent majority of my fellow Americans—I ask for your support.

I pledged in my campaign for the presidency to end the war in a way that we could win the peace. I have initiated a plan of action which will enable me to keep that pledge.

The more support I can have from the American people, the sooner that pledge can be redeemed; for the more divided we are at home, the less likely the enemy is to negotiate at Paris.

In the 1960s, people began to wear their politics on their car bumpers, as these two opposing bumper stickers illustrate.

Moratorium to End the War

On October and November 15, 1969, a coalition of antiwar groups declared a "Moratorium to End the War," during which hundreds of thousands of people in cities across the country gathered to listen to antiwar speeches, participate in discussions, and attend peaceful rallies. The November event drew over 750,000 people to Washington, D.C., while 250,000 people demonstrated in San Francisco on the same day. The Nixon administration was deeply concerned about how to respond, as illustrated by these excerpts from the diary of Chief of staff H. R. Haldeman.

THURSDAY, NOVEMBER 13, 1969

The Vietnam [sic] march started tonight at 6:00. No problems at the White House. Just single file of candle carriers with name placards of war dead. E [John Erlichman; another Nixon aide] and I stayed at the White House all night, he in his office, I in the shelter. Not too bad. Went out and watched them for a while, mostly kids, some very young. Mostly solemn and quiet, a few kooky types. P [resident Nixon] not interested, spent two hours at bowling alley.

FRIDAY, NOVEMBER 14, 1969

(Vietnam) march and mob grew violent tonight as groups tried to march on Vietnamese embassy. Police busted it up with tear gas, but they roamed streets breaking windows, etc. We were in E's office working phones, etc. when P came in about 9:00, stayed until 11:00. Interested in whole process. Had helpful ideas like using helicopters to blow their candles out, etc. (The marchers were all carrying candles in the night as a dramatic gesture for TV.) Very relaxed. Said was like watching an old movie, keep thinking something interesting will happen.

Nixon gave the press corps a geography lesson as he explained his order to invade Cambodia.

Let us be united for peace. Let us also be united against defeat. Because let us understand: North Vietnam cannot defeat or humiliate the United States. Only Americans can do that.

Nixon solved the dilemma of how to escalate the war while claiming to deescalate it, linguistically. He called the 1970 invasion of Cambodia an "incursion," refrained from informing the American people that the United States had been bombing Cambodia for a full year, and claimed that the main goal was to attack the headquarters of the "entire Communist military operation in South Vietnam." Here is an excerpt from his dramatic television address on April 30, 1970, announcing the invasion.

Good evening my fellow Americans:
We take this action not for the purpose of expanding the war into Cambodia but for the purpose of ending the war in Vietnam and winning the just peace we all desire. We have made and we will continue to make every possible effort to end this war through negotiation at the conference table rather than through more fighting on the battlefield. . . .

The action that I have announced tonight puts the leaders of North Vietnam on notice that we will be patient in working for peace; we will be conciliatory at the conference table, but we will not be humiliated. We will not be defeated. We will not allow American men by the thousands to be killed by an enemy from privileged sanctuaries. . . .

If, when the chips are down, the world's most powerful nation, the United States of America, acts like a pitiful, helpless giant, the forces of totalitarianism and anarchy will threaten free nations and free institutions throughout the world.

It is not our power but our will and character that is being tested tonight. . . . I have rejected all political considerations in making this decision. . . . Whether my party gains in November is nothing compared to the lives of 400,000 brave Americans fighting for our country and for the cause of peace and freedom in Vietnam. . . . I would rather be a one-term President and do what I believe is right than to be a two-term President at the cost of seeing America become a second-rate power and to see this Nation accept the first defeat in its proud 190-year history.

Minutes after this speech, student-organized protest demonstrations were under way at Princeton University in New Jersey and Oberlin College in Ohio. Within a few days, strikes and other protests had taken place at scores of colleges and universities throughout the country. On two campuses, Kent State University in Ohio and Jackson State College in Mississippi, the demonstrations turned deadly. President Nixon, who had congratulated the governor of Ohio for having called out some 750 National Guardsmen to restrain the students, established an investigative commission on "campus unrest." In its report, the commission underlines what it takes to be the deeper issues involved at Kent State and other college campuses.

On the whole, American students are not as politically radical as some press reports might suggest. Only three years ago, in the spring of 1967, a Gallup poll of college students found that 49 percent classified themselves as "hawks" on the war in Vietnam. Since that time, there has been a dramatic shift of students' attitudes toward the " December 1969 found that only 20 percent of the students classified themselves as "hawks" while 69 percent classified themselves as "doves." At the same time, 50 percent—as compared to 64 percent of the adult public—

Sometimes there seemed to be a conversation going on between bumper stickers and posters:

A marine ROTC recruiting table is identified by an unwelcome sign in John Jay Hall at Columbia University in 1967. Campuses were sharply divided over the presence of ROTC on campus.

approved of the way President Nixon was handling the situation in Vietnam. . . .

Why do the President and disaffected college youth have trouble "communicating" about Vietnam? At least four factors are at work. First, the President uses words that mean one thing to him but something different to many students. For example, he has emphasized that he and students both want "peace." By "peace," students mean an end to the killing immediately. To them the President seems to mean not that, but a "just peace" and "self-determination for South Vietnam," which they see as probably meaning maintenance of a pro-American regime in Saigon, continued U.S. military presence in Southeast Asia, and whatever military action is necessary to produce these ends.

Exacerbating this difficulty is the belief of many students—shared, it is fair to say, by many nonstudents—that the course we are on has no real chance of success. . . .

Second, what the President regards as successes, students often regard very differently. Reducing the troop level in Vietnam by sometime in 1971 to something over 200,000 men seems to many in Government a formidable achievement. The President so proclaims it. Yet to the young, who face the draft and think on the time scale of youth, these withdrawals seem wholly inadequate. . . . Third, to some students, the President appears not to understand the nature of the crisis that has come over the country. He speaks of "deep divisions" in the country. But "deep divisions" suggests a serious disagreement in a stable society: a matter of different groups holding different opinions. . . . [Students] see not just differences of opinion, but rather the whole social order as being in a state of erosion. . . . Fourth, and this really underlies the other points, the President and some students proceed from vastly different assumptions. The President says, "America has never lost a war," as if "winning" or "losing" were the important consideration. He seems to them to hold attitudes derived from the "cold war," such as the domino theory, and to view Communism in Southeast Asia as a source of danger to America. Wrongly or rightly, many of our best-informed students do not share these assumptions. The President speaks of maintaining "national honor" and implies that this can be done through military power. . . . [Students] see the Vietnam war and its effects at home as obstructing fulfillment of their concept of national honor. Just as an earlier generation fought in World War II to preserve the nation's ideals, they want to end the war to help attain the nation's ideals.

Vietnamization did not in any sense mean an end to American devastation of Vietnam, as the following speech by Democratic Senator Gaylord Nelson of Wisconsin on February 25, 1972, makes clear.

Suppose we took gigantic bulldozers and scraped the land bare of trees and bushes at the rate of 1,000 acres a day or 44 million square feet a day until we had flattened an area the size of Rhode Island, 750,000 acres.

Suppose we flew huge planes over the land and sprayed 100 million pounds of poisonous herbicides on the forests until we had destroyed an area of prime forests the size of Massachusetts or 5 1/2 million acres. . . .

Suppose we flew B-52 bombers over the land, dropping 500 pound bombs until we had dropped almost 3 pounds per person for every man, woman and child on earth—8 billion pounds—and created 23 million craters on the land measuring 26 feet deep and 40 feet in diameter.

Nixon and the Students

Nationwide demonstrations, including the fatal one at Kent State, consumed the White House. Both Nixon and Vice President Spiro Agnew were widely quoted in the press for their negative comments on students (Nixon referred to dissident students as "bums"). Chief of staff H. R. Haldeman recorded daily discussions of how to handle the situation.

THURSDAY, MAY 7, 1970
P[resident Nixon] met with university presidents. . . . Feels very concerned about campus revolt and basically helpless to deal with it. It's now clear that many are looking to him for leadership and to calm it down, and there's really no way he can do it. Also have omnipresent media problem, as they build up everything to look as bad as possible. P said the university presidents were all scared to death, feel that this now includes non-radical students, and agree with Moynihan's theory that the whole university community is now politicized, and there's no way to turn it off. All blame Agnew primarily, then the P's "bums" crack. General feeling is that without Kent State it would not have been so bad, but that even without Cambodia there were a lot of campuses ready to blow.

FRIDAY, MAY 8, 1970
An awful lot of schools closed, a lot of rhetoric, a major threat of violence, etc. . . . All through the day the advice poured in from all sources, as everyone feared the P would either be too belligerent and non-understanding of dissenters, or would be too forgiving and thus lose strength and P leadership. All depends on your point of view. I gave all the pertinent advice on both sides to the P, the hard line mainly from K[Henry Kissinger] who feels we should just let the students tear it for a couple of weeks with no effort at pacification, then hit them hard.

National Guard troops advance on students demonstrating at Kent State University, Ohio, on May 4, 1970. Four students were shot dead. Governor James Rhodes swore that in Ohio he would not "treat the symptoms" but "eradicate the problem."

Suppose the major objective of the bombing is not enemy troops but rather a vague and unsuccessful policy of harassment and territorial denial called pattern or carpet bombing.

Suppose the land destruction involves 80% of the timber forests and 10% of all the cultivated land in the nation.

We would consider such results a monumental catastrophe. That is what we have done to our ally, South Vietnam. . . .

Quite frankly, I am unable adequately to describe the horror of what we have done there.

There is nothing in the history of warfare to compare with it. A "scorched earth" policy has been a tactic of warfare throughout history but never has a land been so massively altered and mutilated that vast areas can never be used again or even inhabited by man or animal. . . .

If they could see and understand the result, they would not draw the lines or send the bombers.

If Congress knew and understood, we would not appropriate the money. If the president of the United States knew and understood, he would stop it in 30 minutes.

If the people of America knew and understood, they would remove from office those responsible for it if they could ever find out who is responsible. But they will never know, because nobody knows. . . .

The cold, hard and cruel irony of it all is that South Vietnam would have been better off losing to Hanoi than winning with us. Now she faces the worst of all possible worlds with much of her land destroyed and her chances of independent survival after we leave in grave doubt at best.

Bombing Hanoi to the Bargaining Table

Peace talks in Paris, which began at the end of the Johnson administration in May 1969, broke down in October after President Thieu made it clear he would not go along with the agreements reached between Secretary of State Henry Kissinger and the North Vietnamese. In December 1972, the Nixon administration began its massive "Christmas bombing" campaign against Hanoi. In January 1973, talks resumed and an agreement was reached. The Nixon administration claimed, at the time and later, that it had bombed Hanoi back to the bargaining table, although the terms reached in October were virtually identical to those finally agreed upon.

Christmas Bombing

Worst of all has been the failure of a single person in the United States government to break with a policy that many must know history will judge a crime against humanity.

To send B-52s against populous areas such as Haiphong or Hanoi could have only one sole purpose: terror. It was the response of a man so overwhelmed by his sense of inadequacy and frustration that he had to strike out, punish, destroy. . . .

The American imagination has evidently ceased to be stirred by the facts of bombing. When people have not lived under bombs, as few Americans have, they perhaps cannot imagine the continuous fear. They may not understand that bombs dropped in cities and villages kill human beings indiscriminately, the innocent with the wicked. They do not see themselves caught even hundreds of yards from the center of a B-52 raid, the concussion crushing their lungs or spewing out their insides.

—Columnist Anthony Lewis in response to the "Christmas Bombing." *New York Times,* December 23, 1972

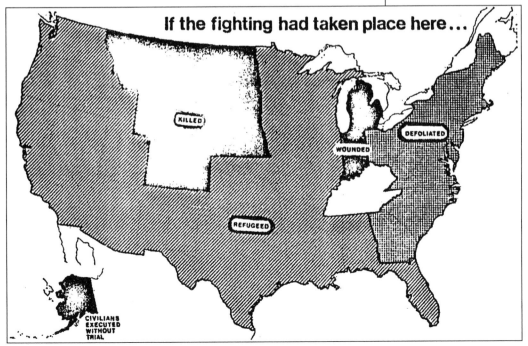

By superimposing the damage done to Vietnam on a map of the United States, this graphic, seen origianlly in Win magazine, makes concrete the extent of defoliated land, and the number of refugees, wounded, dead, and executed without trial.

A poster pointing out that funds intended for President Johnson's war on poverty had been diverted to the war in Vietnam. Johnson had hoped to be able to fund both guns and butter; in the end, the guns won.

They're eating us out of house, home, city, school, medical care and clean air.

They're President Thieu and Vice President Ky, the military rulers of South Vietnam.

This year they're tapping us for about $13 billion to help fight their war. That's enough money to build 2,000 high schools, 10,000 low-rent apartments, provide hospital facilities for 165,000 patients, and increase the pollution control program by ten times.

Even if we withdraw all our troops, we will still give South Vietnam $2.5 billion in military and economic aid. That's as much money as we give to all other countries combined.

Maybe it's time we paid less attention to soothing phrases like "Vietnamization" and "peace-time economy" and paid more attention to the figures.

Write to your Representative and ask for a copy of the Federal budget. Tell him where you want to spend the $10.5 billion we'd save by getting out of Vietnam.

Help unsell the war.
Box 903 F.D.R. Station, New York, N.Y. 10022

The Nixon administration, more secretive than most, reached private agreements with both the government of South Vietnam and the North Vietnamese. In order to overcome President Thieu's reluctance to accept the Paris peace accords, Nixon wrote to him directly, promising that the United States would respond with "full force" should Hanoi violate the terms of the settlement. And, in a secret agreement, Nixon promised Hanoi $2.5 billion in reconstruction aid. Watergate saved Nixon from having to make good on either promise. In this letter to President Thieu, Nixon makes it clear

that the South Vietnamese had little choice but to accept the agreement or continue the war entirely on their own.

This will acknowledge your letter of December 20, 1972. There is nothing substantial that I can add to my many previous messages, including my December 17 letter, which clearly stated my opinions and intentions. With respect to the question of North Vietnamese troops, we will again present your views to the Communists as we have done vigorously at every other opportunity in the negotiations. The result is certain to be once more the rejection of our position. We have explained to you repeatedly why we believe the problem of North Vietnamese troops is manageable under the agreement, and I see no reason to repeat all the arguments.

We will proceed next week in Paris along the lines that General Haig explained to you. Accordingly, if the North Vietnamese meet our concerns on the two outstanding substantive issues in the agreement, concerning the DMZ and the method of signing, and if we can arrange acceptable supervisory machinery, we will proceed to conclude the settlement. The gravest consequences would then ensue if your government settlement chose to reject the agreement and split off from the United States. As I said in my December 17 letter, "I am convinced that your refusal to join us would be an invitation to disaster—to the loss of all that we together have fought for over the past decade. It would be inexcusable above all because we will have lost a just and honorable alternative."

As we enter this new round of talks, I hope that our countries will now show a united front. It is imperative for our common objectives that your government take no further actions that complicate our task and would make more difficult the acceptance of the settlement by all parties. We will keep you informed of the negotiations in Paris through daily briefings of Ambassador Lam.

I can only repeat what I have so often said: The best guarantee for the survival of South Vietnam is the unity of our two countries which would be gravely jeopardized if you persist in your present course. The actions of our Congress since its return have clearly borne out the many warnings we have made.

Should you decide, as I trust you will, to go with us, you have my assurance of continued assistance in the post-settlement period and that we will respond with full force should the settlement be violated by North Vietnam. So once more I conclude with an appeal to you to close ranks with us.

The Pentagon Papers

In 1967 Secretary of Defense Robert McNamara, increasingly disturbed by the course of the war, asked a group of his aides, including Daniel Ellsberg, to prepare a history of the U.S. involvement in Vietnam. The 47-volume result drew on classified material from the archives of the Department of Defense, the State Department, and the CIA, tracing U.S. policy from 1945 to 1968.

Working on it had turned Ellsberg against the war. In 1971 Ellsberg, now an employee of the RAND corporation (a private, federally funded research corporation), and a colleague, Anthony Russo, secretly copied large sections of the report. After several senators refused to have anything to do with the matter, they handed the collection over to Neil Sheehan of the New York Times, *which began to publish articles by reporters based on the documents as well as some of the documents themselves. Attorney General John Mitchell demanded that the newspaper stop and return the documents to the Pentagon. When the* Times *refused, Mitchell got a court order restraining publication. Ellsberg then passed some of the papers to the* Washington Post, *which immediately published articles based on the material, though not the documents themselves. Ultimately the case was argued before the Supreme Court, which ruled in favor of the press. In this interview excerpt, Daniel Ellsberg reflects on his decision.*

When I look back at my actions to end the war, I wish I had done in 1964 or 1965 what I did do five years later: *go to Congress, tell the truth, with documents.* From my first day in the Pentagon—August 4, 1964—I witnessed lies about U.S. provocations and imaginary torpedoes in the Tonkin Gulf. I became a participant in secret plans to escalate the war as soon as President Johnson won in a landslide by promising voters just the opposite. If I (and others) had done then what I did later, the war could have been averted.

That's a heavy thought to bear, and I'm still carrying it. It's easy to say that it simply didn't occur to me at the time. Like so many others I put personal loyalty to the President above all else—above loyalty to the Constitution and above obligation to law, to truth to Americans and to humankind. I was wrong. . . . Telling the truth can have a power more than worthy of the risk.

Chapter 8

After the War

There are no uniform legacies to the long, hard war in Vietnam. The biggest divide is between what the war has left behind in the United States and what effect it had on Indochina. The best introduction to this topic may be a simple listing of statistics.

Over the course of the war, 58,135 U.S. soldiers died and 304,704 were wounded. There were 6,665 amputees, and more than 33,000 men came home paralyzed to one degree or another. As in all wars, those who participated in direct combat have continued to suffer from their experience. In the Civil War, this was called "soldier's heart," in World War I, "shell shock," in World War II and Korea, "battle fatigue," and in Vietnam, "post-traumatic stress disorder" (PTSD). Some 500,000 to 800,000 veterans have been diagnosed with varying levels of PTSD and continue to be treated at Veterans Administration hospitals across the country.

For many families the war will never end. Their relatives continue to be listed as "missing in action," and although there is no evidence that they remain alive or incarcerated in Vietnam, the hopes of their families are expressed in a fierce insistence that continues to trouble relations between the United States and Vietnam.

The war cost American taxpayers $168 billion in direct military expenditures, and if one adds the amount of military and civilian aid to the government of South Vietnam and indirect military costs, the figure rises to $2 trillion. Another cost—one that cannot be quantified, however—is the widespread sense of disillusionment with the government of the country, a conviction on the part of many citizens that their representatives cannot be trusted not to lie. The internal divisions caused by the war were bitter, and they linger to this day, expressed by some in a hostility to government as such and by others in resistance to sending U.S. troops abroad for almost any purpose.

On April 21, 1975, President Thieu bade farewell to the people of South Vietnam in a three-hour televised speech in which he berated the United States for its "perfidy." Five days later, along with 15 tons of baggage, Thieu left Saigon for Taiwan and later the United States.

'THANKS A LOT'

An editorial cartoon in the Miami Daily News *commented on the end of the war and its legacy for the Vietnamese—in this case, a land scarred with bomb craters.*

The Vietnamese statistics reflect the disparity in firepower between the United States and its enemies and the fact that the war was fought on Vietnamese soil. Some estimates of combined military and civilian deaths put the figure as high as 3.8 million people. More modest figures are no less stark: 2 million dead and 4 million wounded. The United States had dropped four times as many bombs on Indochina as it had expended in the combined European and Pacific theaters of World War II. This comes to a destructive force of some 600 Hiroshima-size bombs, leaving Vietnam pockmarked by some 20 million craters. The land suffered in other ways: 18 million gallons of Agent Orange were dropped or sprayed on 4.5 million acres between 1962 and 1971 to clear foliage in which guerrillas might take refuge, as well as to destroy food crops that might feed them. The cancer and genetic disorders for which Agent Orange is responsible continue to harm both the Americans who were exposed to it and the Vietnamese whose crops and water sources were poisoned.

The war caused division among the American people; but it was caused by divisions among Vietnamese. After the war, Hanoi sent those who had served the Saigon government to "reeducation camps" that dealt out more punishment than "reeducation." More than 400,000 people were held in some 100 camps and at least 40,000 remained incarcerated for many years, although all were released by 1988.

The most visible postwar phenomenon was the flight of hundreds of thousands of Vietnamese, under conditions of great hardship. Their reasons for leaving varied: some feared the reeducation camps; others were ethnic Chinese who had lived in Vietnam for generations but nevertheless felt endangered as relations between China and Vietnam deteriorated in the late 1970s. Many of those who emigrated believed the new regime would discriminate against them because of their religion or their family backgrounds. And there were, as well, "economic refugees" who left Vietnam as the economic situation steadily worsened under the triple hardships of an American embargo instituted immediately after the fall of Saigon in April 1975, the devastation caused by almost 30 years of continuous warfare, and the counterproductive effect of inept economic measures.

Although the source of discontent was different, many Vietnamese felt as disillusioned with their government as Americans did with theirs.

Since the lifting of the embargo and the normalization of relations between the two countries in 1995, Vietnam has begun to recover economically. Nguyen Duy, a Vietnamese poet, perhaps speaks for all those affected by the Vietnam–American war. Standing before the ancient ruins of Cambodia's Angkor Wat, he reflected:

> if stone can be so shattered, what of human life?
> Oh stone,
> let me inscribe a plea for peace.
> In the end, in every war,
> whoever won, the people always lost.

Looking Back

Larry Heinemann is one of an extraordinary group of veterans who became writers. His first novel, *Close Quarters*, was a powerful account of combat; his second, *Paco's Story*, won the 1987 National Book Award. In this essay for a collection of reminiscences, Heinemann reflects on the nature of war, the divisions it caused in the country, and offers an answer the question "could the United States have won?"

The Vietnam War was a benchmark of American history if there ever was one. It was a cusp. A strangely shaped event through which the Vietnam survivors—the whole country, for that matter—was extruded. We lost our naivete—had it ripped out of our throats; had it beat out of us most dramatically—understanding finally that the government had betrayed us with a program of lies. Lyndon Johnson's (and for that matter Richard Nixon's) was a government of selfish, arrogant old men, jolly well ready to eat its own young, both overseas and back here, to preserve its own shabby honor and specious dignity. Nixon's "peace with honor" is as hollow and shallow and laughable a phrase as Chamberlain's "peace in our time." In its own way the Vietnam War was as extraordinary, divisive, and evocative as the Civil War—with its senseless bloodfeud, self-destruction, draft riots, and eager but doomed young volunteers. The Vietnam War was a dirty, sloppy, ballbreaking, ugly, grueling, mean-spirited, and hateful business. And we—the soldiers in the field—learned to hate people on sight for the slant of their eyes and black pants they wore.

Parenthetically, there is nowadays circulating the oddly revised notion that the United States could have won the war. Where did this notion come from! Certainly not from any 11-Bravo grunt I know. To say we could have won the war is to say that we didn't fill our hearts with enough hate; didn't napalm or

Fuzzy History

While many Americans felt strongly about Vietnam, they actually knew very little about its history. President Ronald Reagan was no exception, as his remarks at an April 1982 news conference indicate.

If I recall correctly, when France gave up Indochina as a colony, the leading nations of the world met in Geneva with regard to helping those colonies become independent nations. And since North and South Vietnam had been, previous to colonization, two separate countries, provisions were made that these two countries could by a vote of all their people together, decide whether they wanted to be one country or not.

And there wasn't anything surreptitious about it, that when Ho Chi Minh refused to participate in such an election—and there was provision that people of both countries could cross the border and live in the other country if they wanted to. And when they began leaving by the thousands and thousands from North Vietnam to South Vietnam, Ho Chi Minh closed the border and again violated that part of the agreement.

And openly, our country sent military advisers there to help a country which had been a colony have such things as a national security force, an army, you might say, or a military to defend itself. And they were doing this, if I recall correctly, also in civilian clothes, no weapons, until they began being blown up where they lived and walking down the street by people riding by on bicycles and throwing pipe bombs at them. And then they were permitted to carry sidearms or wear uniforms. But it was totally a program until John F. Kennedy—when these attacks and forays became so great that John F. Kennedy authorized the sending in of a division of Marines.

And that was the first move toward combat troops in Vietnam.

strafe or frag them hard enough; didn't Zippo enough hooches or turn enough of their women into whores; didn't bomb them with B-52 air strikes into small enough pieces far enough back into the stone age—the bomb craters as big as city house lots. . . .

I was drafted, submitted to conscription with what can only be described as soul-deadening dread, and did my tour of Tay Ninh Province (1967–68) on an armored personnel carrier in the mechanized infantry. We rode roughshod over the country around Tay Ninh. . . . It seemed especially ominous and foreboding to find ruined, long abandoned French trucks and tanks and field pieces in the jungle—abundant foliage growing out of the turrets and hatches and the horsehair seat cushions. We weren't so bone-numb exhausted and grunt-work stupid that the inference was lost on us: This is what happened to the French, and they hadn't been in Southeast Asia since 1954, what the hell are we doing here! . . .

You could stand buck naked in the middle of a village street and piss in plain sight of a hundred people, and as long as you were a GI with a rifle and a steel pot, no one dared say boo. Of course it's gross. We tracked them down like dogs and shot them on sight and measured battlefield success by the particular institution of the body count, as if the corpses were so many road kills. Standing naked taking a whiz in public seems the least of our atrocities; such were the broad and generous permissions in the field. . . .

The war was unwinnable in any case. Such was the Vietnamese extraordinary ambition to rid their country of foreigners that we would have had to kill them all and burn their country to the ground. . . .

Our most vulnerable and trusting impulses had been betrayed—squeezed out of us, burned out—by a solid year's tour. By a government that would rather kill us all than admit a mistake. We were worse than so many numbers, worse still than so many bricks in the wall, we were so much meat on the slab to be butchered. . . .

Vietnam veterans as a rule feel used, wasted, and then dumped: many a veteran still harbors a bitterness and distrust of authority that in the years since has crusted over and hardened, but will never be ameliorated. There will always be dark places on my heart because of an almost unreasonable bitterness. It is that undeniable perception of betrayal which informs so much of the Vietnam veterans' attitudes and self-image. We are not victims and we are not heroes; there is nothing ennobling or enriching or manful about the infantry. . . .

On another subject. The Vietnam War divided a generation of men. I was once told by an editor of a prominent literary magazine that he felt he had missed something by not having gone to Vietnam: he assumed it was part of his manhood he missed, what used to be called a "rite of passage." He also talked about a missed literary opportunity, which I think was selfish of him, if not a little sad. I told him quite honestly that he saved himself a great deal of grief. There are those days when I would trade both my novels for these twenty years of grief. The men of my generation who opposed the war had every good reason to oppose it—their morality and the sincerity of their strong personal feeling are not in question.

I don't know that any reasonable, sensible person thinks the Vietnam War was a good and righteous undertaking, but it is crucial that we come to understand the war as an event and expression of our national character, and accept our responsibility. Now we have to discover what it was—this epoch of arrogant greed and self-destruction—and be honest with ourselves.

Former Secretary of Defense Robert McNamara, whom many historians consider one of the principal architects of the war, expressed second thoughts in his 1995 memoir, *In Retrospect*.

This is the book I planned never to write.

Although pressed repeatedly for over a quarter of a century to add my views on Vietnam to the public record, I hesitated for fear that I might appear self-serving, defensive, or vindictive, which I wished to avoid at all costs. Perhaps I hesitated also because it is hard to face one's mistakes. But something changed my attitude and willingness to speak. I am responding not to a desire to get out my personal story but rather to a wish to put before the American people why their government and its leaders behaved as they did and what we may learn from that experience. . . .

I know that, to this day, many political leaders and scholars in the United States and abroad argue that the Vietnam War actually helped contain the spread of Communism in South and East Asia. Some argue that it hastened the end of the Cold War. But I also know that the war caused terrible damage to America. No doubt exists in my mind about that. None. I want to look at Vietnam in hindsight, not in any way to obscure my own and others' errors of judgment and their egregious costs but to show the full range of pressures and the lack of knowledge that existed at the time.

"When Johnny comes marching home again hurrah, hurrah."

John Diakoyani
Hoboken, N.J.

Stop the crippling. Stop the killing. Stop the war.
Write, wire or call your congressman today.
Help Unsell The War, Box 903, F.D.R. Station, New York, N.Y. 10022

A poster of a wounded veteran, John Diakoyani of Hoboken, N.J., reflects on the end of the war and its legacy for Americans.

I want to put Vietnam in context.

We of the Kennedy and Johnson administrations who participated in the decisions on Vietnam acted according to what we thought were the principles and traditions of this nation. We made our decisions in light of those values.

Yet we were wrong, terribly wrong.

Reaction to McNamara's book ranged from sympathy for his expression of remorse to anger at his long silence. R. Drummond Ayres Jr. reported on veterans' views for the *New York Times*.

Reaction to the former Defense Secretary's revised views . . . has mostly been relentlessly negative, with little credence or charity accorded Mr. McNamara's comment that "we were wrong, terribly wrong."

The criticism has come from just about every quarter—combat veterans, former colleagues in Government, hawks, doves, editorialists and, of course, the children of the 60s who took to the streets and to the grassy grounds outside Mr. McNamara's Pentagon window to noisily, sometimes violently, protest "McNamara's war." . . .

In particular, many veterans bitterly fault Mr. McNamara, publicly a hawk's hawk throughout his Pentagon days, for his most striking admission: that he knew as early as 1967 that involvement in the conflict was a catastrophic mistake but that he could not bring himself to say so until almost three decades later.

"It sure would have been helpful in May of 1967, when I volunteered for Vietnam, if he had said then that the war was unwinnable," Max Cleland, who lost both legs in Vietnam and afterward served as head of the Veterans Administration, said in an interview. . . .

"McNamara went to the World Bank," Mr. Cleland concluded, "while a lot of other people went to their graves." . . .

Martin Kaplan of Seattle, who was sent to Vietnam in 1969, is still angry about the war, and the McNamara book has only exacerbated that anger. "I don't see McNamara's revelations doing any good for anyone," Mr. Kaplan said as he and several other veterans sat together . . . watching the former Defense Secretary discuss his book on the television show *Prime Time Live*. "There's a sense of betrayal. To him it was just an intellectual exercise. And he was called one of the best and brightest?"

Most of the other veterans sitting with Mr. Kaplan also expressed anger about Mr. McNamara's revelation. But then, with some wiping away tears as the former Secretary spoke, himself in tears, they offered an unusual perspective, one that while it was not forgiving was nevertheless understanding.

"We're seeing another Vietnam veteran dealing with his grief and guilt," said Lee Raaen, a former Army draftee who was shipped to Vietnam in 1970 and now is a Seattle lawyer. "But I suppose I could say, from a historical standpoint, 'It's about time.'"

Few of McNamara's colleagues in the government agreed with his recantation. Former Secretary of State Dean Rusk was especially unapologetic.

Since leaving office in 1969, I have been offered many chances to present a mea culpa on Vietnam, but I have not availed myself of those opportunities. I thought the principal decisions made by President Kennedy and President Johnson were the right decisions at the time they were made. I supported their decisions. There is nothing I can say now that would diminish my share of responsibility for the events of those years. I live with that, and others can make of it what they will.

I have not apologized for my role in Vietnam, for the simple reason that I believed in the principles that underlay our commitment to South Vietnam and why we fought that war. As a private citizen I believe in those principles today. The withdrawal of American troops did not bring genuine peace to Southeast Asia. . . .

Could the Vietnam War have been won? I think so, if we could have maintained solidarity on the home front and if we could have accepted "winning" as defined by the Kennedy and Johnson administrations: preventing North Vietnam's takeover of South Vietnam by force.

Personally I hoped and expected the North Vietnamese would realize that they could not overrun South Vietnam militarily and that when they came to this realization, we and they would find some way to conclude the war, negotiate a cease-fire, and work towards a political settlement along the lines of the status quo ante. But they were encouraged to stick it out, and they eventually got it all. However, I am convinced that our men in uniform carried out their mission: to prevent North Vietnam from seizing South Vietnam by force. It wasn't until we pulled our forces out and Congress cut off supplies that North Vietnam overran the South. . . .

[T]he real journalistic lessons to be learned from the belated publication of McNamara's book are these: The greatest failure of American journalism in the Vietnam years was not on location in Vietnam, where in fact it was generally quite good. . . . Rather, the failure could be found in Washington, where all kinds of reporters who should have known better accepted the hierarchical version of the truth and did not try to penetrate that myth.

—David Halberstam, "Vietnam: Why We Missed the Story," Washington Post, May 1995

At left, a downtrodden cemetery for soldiers of the losing Army of the Republic of Vietnam. At right, an orderly and reverent Vietnamese National War Cemetery honoring the victorious dead troops. Both of these cemeteries are at Bien Hoa. The winners and losers of the war are apparent in the appearance of their memorial graveyards.

As secretary of state I made two serious mistakes with respect to Vietnam. First, I overestimated the patience of the American people, and second, I underestimated the tenacity of the North Vietnamese. They took frightful casualties. In relation to our own population, their total casualties throughout the war were roughly equivalent to ten million American casualties. . . .

My other mistake was overestimating the patience of the American people. As a people we Americans are very impatient about war, and God bless us for that. Americans, as do ordinary people at the grass roots in every country, strongly prefer peace and abhor war. The trouble is, in a democracy this yearning for peace gets full expression, offering opportunities for totalitarian regimes to misinterpret American policy and underestimate what we are prepared to do. . . .

Should the United States have made a stand in South Vietnam? Undoubtedly Presidents Kennedy and Johnson might have decided differently with the full benefit of hindsight—but that opportunity never comes. History will makes its own judgment, but I personally believed the American commitment to South Vietnam was the right decision and have never changed my mind.

On Veterans Day, 1982, the American dead of Vietnam were remembered at the dedication of a memorial built through the efforts of veterans themselves. The selection of an appropriate design renewed the bitter divisions of the war itself. The chosen architect, 21-year-old Maya Ying Lin, had

designed a simple, elegant structure: two black granite walls bearing, in gold leaf, the names of the fallen. Protest was almost immediate. The design was thought to be unpatriotic, a "black gash" in the earth. The protesters raised money and a more traditional memorial was built facing the wall itself: a group of three life-sized soldiers in front of an American flag. The Vietnam Veterans' Memorial is the single most visited site in Washington, D.C., and the ambiguity of its form has meant that its meaning is in the eye of the individual beholder.

Bruce Weigl, poet and Vietnam veteran, attended the dedication ceremonies for the memorial in 1982, and reported on the occasion in *The Nation*.

It is the first national gathering of Vietnam veterans, a reception sponsored by *Stars and Stripes*, the AmVets and the Vietnam Veterans of America. They arrive in small groups all evening, the way they'd come back to the country so long ago: at night, in the rain, in small groups. Someone believed then it was possible to slip us all back from the war into the spaces we'd left a year before. It turns out it was not possible. It turns out many of us have hurt all this time.

By 9 o'clock Friday night the room is packed with Vietnam veterans, World War II veterans, Army nurses, politicians, the maimed, the curious, the angry and bitter, the hapless, the gung-ho warriors of every war, real, imagined and of our collective memory. We are given $5000 worth of beer and one another and

The Vietnam Veterans Memorial in Washington, D.C. is notoriously difficult to capture in a photograph; this one illustrates how different it is from most war memorials. It is without any reference to heroism; one descends to the wall of names, as if into a grave.

are cordoned off from the world for the night. We spill out into the streets and huddle together in squad-sized groups. . . .

I don't know why we came here. We are so different now. At the Agent Orange hearing in the Cannon Building, a man from Cleveland stood up and addressed the distinguished panel of experts. Sobbing, he told the story of his child dying from brain disease and the story of his own long suffering as a result of exposure to the monster Dioxin, the head's revenge on the body. He cried and he pleaded and he asked only for help. It is fifteen years and no one has helped him. And he wondered how long he has to wait. "Let the world decide," he said. One by one they stood and testified, each in his different pain, all with the lost years in common. . . .

Later, I stood in a rain away from everyone with Gary Beikirch. He is a big, shy and humble man who won the Medal of Honor for what he did in Vietnam. When he came back from the war, Gary moved to the Maine mountains to heal. He had already lived a thousand lives and he was tired. Two years after his return, they called him down to Washington and Nixon pinned the medal on his chest. Nixon, dear God: Gary went home and put the medal away as he had tried to put away the nightmare it stood for.

We shivered in the rain. The sense that something good was happening around us caught us both by surprise. It seemed possible that the ghosts could be driven finally from our hearts. And Gary, who doesn't tell his pain easily, opened up. He played it all back so carefully and so clearly I could hardly stop myself from shaking. He was a senior medic for a Special Forces A-team on the Laotian border attacked on April Fool's night by three North Vietnamese regiments. Twice wounded, his legs numb from shrapnel lodged near his spine, he dragged himself from soldier to soldier, child to child, to try to stop the bleeding, until he was wounded again, his stomach torn open, and he still went into fire again and again, tending the others until the pain overcame him.

I think we came, without really knowing it, to make the memorial our wailing wall. We came to find the names of those we lost in the war, as if by tracing the letters cut into the granite we could find what was left of ourselves. It turns out that, beyond all the petty debates over the monument, no veteran could turn his back on the terrible grace of Maya Lin's wall and the names of the 57,939 who died or disappeared in Vietnam from July 1959 to May 1975: America's longest, most vicious sin. . . .

Fewer marched this cold Saturday morning than died or were wounded during those sixteen years. The parade was quiet and simple; it all seemed so quickly to pass away. Sadly, this is all many Vietnam veterans ever wanted: to be let back into the lives of our families and friends, to have a small parade at home, a ritual old as war, a necessary, essential lie. There is little doubt that the suffering here and in Vietnam will continue for a long time while the bureaucracies argue over blame. But in the cold wind blowing off the reflecting pool beyond Maya Lin's wall, you could pick your head up again; you could believe that you had finally come home.

For several years, a group of American officials active in the Kennedy and Johnson administrations have met with their counterparts in Hanoi to discuss the history they all lived through and to some extent made. Both Vietnamese and American historians joined these sessions. The discussions were recorded and published; these excerpts are from the discussion about the Geneva Accords and the period immediately before and after those meetings. Chester Cooper was a CIA analyst for Southeast Asia from 1953 to 1963 and a member of the National Security Council from 1963 to 1966. Col. Herbert Y. Shandler served two tours of duty in Vietnam and is currently a professor at the National Defense University in Washington, D.C. Luu Van Loi was an army officer in the war against France and then became a member of the Ministry of Foreign Affairs. Luu Doan Huyn joined the Vietnam People's Army in 1945 and later served in the Foreign Ministry. Both are leading historians.

LUU DOAN HUYN: In 1947, Ho Chi Minh sent Vice Minister Pham Ngoc Thach to Bangkok to explain to your embassy about the Vietnamese policy. Later on, in 1948, Mr. Thach invited a U.S. representative to visit our base area to see our resistance—to see for himself—what we were fighting for and so on. But the invitation was refused.

Born in the U.S.A.

To Bruce Springsteen's distress, in 1984, both Presidential candidates, Walter Mondale and Ronald Reagan, tried to appropriate his ballad to working-class veterans, "Born in the U.S.A." The song, as Springsteen sings it, is hardly celebratory.

Born down in a dead man's town
The first kick I took was when I hit the ground
You end up like a dog that's been beat too
  much
Till you spend half your life just covering up

Chorus:

Born in the U.S.A.
I was born in the U.S.A.
I was born in the U.S.A.
Born in the U.S.A.
Got in a little hometown jam
so they put a rifle in my hand
Sent me off to a foreign land
to go and kill the yellow man

Chorus

Come back home to the refinery
Hiring man says "son if it was up to me"
Went down to see my V.A. man
He said "son don't you understand now"
Had a brother at Khe Sanh
fighting off the Viet Cong
They're still there
He's all gone
He had a woman he loved in Saigon
I got a picture of him in her arms now
Down in the shadow of the penitentiary
Out by the gas fires of the refinery
I'm ten years burning down the road
Nowhere to run ain't got nowhere to go

In 1949, we were preparing the trip of President Ho Chi Minh to China to seek help. At that time, a U.S. journalist asked: "Can Vietnam be neutral like Switzerland?" . . . Ho Chi Minh's answer was, "Why not?"

Luu then acknowledges that in the 1940s, the U.S. was "more or less neutral. . . . Maybe 80% neutral. Okay. To us 80% neutral was acceptable."

But then, you know, in 1950, you discarded all these correct and sensible views . . . . and you said that the struggle of the DRV is a part of the Chinese expansionist game in Asia. There you were wrong. If I may say so, you were not only wrong, but you had, so to speak, lost your minds. Vietnam a part of the Chinese expansionist game in Asia? For anyone who knows the history of Indochina, this is incomprehensible. This is why I say: This is the "original sin"—if I may use the Catholic term—the "original sin" of the United States. . . .

COL. HERBERT SCHANDLER: You have stated a Vietnamese view of this very eloquently. As I was listening to you speak . . . I could sense how confusing it must have been, in 1950, for you to try to figure out why this country that you knew almost nothing about, the United States, had for some reason decided to become your enemy.

But—and this seems to be something that was very hard for you in Vietnam to grasp, for obvious reasons—the United States was taking a world view of all these issues. The Iron Curtain was falling all across Europe. This was shocking. We had fought a bloody war in Europe, and had won, only to have half of Europe reconquered by a totalitarian system. Communism, we felt, had to be stopped. The Iron Curtain then fell in Asia in 1954 with the armistice in Korea and with the Geneva Accords. Like Chet Cooper, I remember the 1950s and Chet is right: Sometimes it looked to us we were on the losing side of history.

CHESTER COOPER: So the question is: What was it that made you think in this period [1954] that the United States was your enemy? Was it propaganda from the Soviets and Chinese? Was it Dulles? Was it something else? . . .

LUU VAN LOI: Our calculations and judgments were based on this fact, which we saw every day in our country: The U.S. was intervening in Vietnam, replacing the French imperialists, providing critical support for Ngo Dinh Diem, and had thus become, by these means, the enemy of the Vietnamese people!

Therefore, Mr. Cooper, I am afraid I fail to see how, or in what way, we were wrong in our assessment of the U.S. That is my answer. Does this answer satisfy you?

CHESTER COOPER: Not quite. I think you are reading too much backwards into the history we are discussing. Yes, of course, eventually we became enemies, as we well know. But I am telling you authoritatively, as a member of the U.S. government at the time we are talking about, and as one who dealt every day with these issues. That you were wrong in your assessment then, in the mid-1950s. Wrong, wrong, wrong! We had made no such decision to intervene. But—

A farmer rides his water buffalo in a field in which the fuselage of a plane seems to have been planted. The marks of war and the fact of peace still characterize Vietnam today.

and this is the critical point, I think—because you assumed that we were hostile, and were seeking to destroy you, then you did things, and you made statements, that appeared to us to confirm the views of people like John Foster Dulles that you were our mortal enemy. . . .

LUU DOAN HUYNH: But really, your bullets are the killers of our people. We see that this is America's gift to Vietnam— allowing the French to kill our people. This is the most convincing evidence we have of America's loyalties in this affair. So how can we conclude that you are not our enemy? That is impossible. How can we believe that?

So you see, we understand all your arguments about U.S. interests with the French and so on. We believe Mr. Chester Cooper when he says that he did not consider Vietnam an enemy. But please try to understand me when I say: Blood speaks with a terrible voice.

CHESTER COOPER: . . . I think it's fair to say we wished [Diem] well. He inherited a very difficult situation in the South, and we were amazed at the extent to which he was able to solidify his control. We gave him no direct military help that I can recall. We did provide some economic assistance because the South was in difficult shape. . . .

LUU DOAN HUYN: . . . But from our point of view, this is what happened. Already in 1955 Diem began executing people, lots of people, all sorts of people. . . . Diem's security forces were trained in the U.S. And there were many other things that indicated to us that Diem—as the U.S.'s puppet—was taking orders from the U.S. Now Mr. Chester Cooper says that the orders to kill our people in 1955 did not come from Washington. Okay. But how could we know this? He was your guy, and he was killing our people. You see, blood again—blood speaks loudly when you are the one who is bleeding.

Legacies

Duong Van Mai grew up in an extended family in Vietnam, divided, as so many families were, by politics and war. From 1963 to 1968 she worked for the RAND Corporation in Saigon interviewing prisoners of war. She left Vietnam for the United States in 1973, and in 1993 she returned to Vietnam to visit those relatives who had stayed on. This excerpt is from her autobiography, which is also a history of her family.

I felt anxious before I left, unsure of how [my sisters] would receive me after decades of silence. I also hoped that the return to a Vietnam now at peace would finally dispel the images of war that had haunted me since I left in 1973, so that I could take back with me to California the certainty that the sorrows I knew were really of the past. As I spied the green Vietnamese countryside beneath the fuselage, I was overwhelmed with emotion, and memories of battles and deaths flashed through my mind. . . .

Throughout my stay in the South, I would have to constantly adjust my memory of war to the reality of peace. . . .During the drive into the city [from the airport], I felt even more lost. Saigon had changed in those twenty years; houses now stood where there had been empty lots. The traffic was heavy, and I saw the normal scenes of a big city life, unmarred by signs of war. I felt happy, but could not communicate my feelings to Yen [her sister], for whom peace had become routine and unremarkable. . . .

I had to coax Thang [another sister] and Hau [her brother-in-law]—and later, my other relatives in Vietnam—to reminisce about the war, which had become distant to them. They preferred to focus on the present

Two out of these three generations of Vietnamese were born into war. The population has grown from nearly 53 million in 1979 to more than 78 million at the end of 2000. One census cites 33.5 percent of the population under the age of 14 years old.

and on the opportunity to improve their lives, as the economy took off with the influx of foreign capital. When I could talk them into remembering the war, they would marvel at its ferocity and their luck in surviving its violence. Those who had fought on the side of the communists were at times nostalgic, recalling the noble sense of mission and the solidarity of purpose of those bygone days. Although they had suffered, they saw no point in dwelling on the past and nursing their resentment against those that had fought on the other side. Those who had been on the losing side were nostalgic for the old days but reconciled to the new state of things and trying to make the best of it. . . .

Outside Saigon, I saw other signs of renewal. Driving to the seaport of Vung Tau, I did not see refugee huts lining the road, but new brick houses rising in the distance. In the Iron Triangle of Cu Chi, bombed, shelled, and defoliated, nature had taken over, and saplings were turning into mature trees and obliterating many of the craters. Passing by a cemetery with 10,000 headstones marking the tombs of Viet Cong who had fallen in battle, I knew that the scars of war were still there, but no longer haunting the living.

After this visit with family in Saigon, Mai Elliott went to visit relatives in Hanoi.

To my surprise, my relatives in the North, whom I had not met or could scarcely remember, welcomed me warmly. Luc [a cousin], now retired from the army and working for a small travel agency, told me his life story with pride and a sense of humor, although he also steered clear of any criticism of the government. He seemed happy, spending his time squiring French tourists to the old Dien Bien Phu battle site, and American visitors down the highway that runs along the coast to Saigon, passing the Vinh Linh area, where he used to fire at American planes. To me, he exemplified the let-bygones-be-bygones spirit of the Vietnamese, rubbing shoulders with people from countries he had once fought. . . .

As my plane took off one fall morning from Hanoi, I looked out of my window and felt a sense of peace and closure. I had renewed family bonds unbroken by time and war, and I had reconnected with my roots and my native soil. I had seen my relatives put the past behind them and move on, stirred once again by hope rather than by fear of bullets and bombs. I had seen Vietnam, the land of two million war dead, become once again the land of the living. And I was taking back with me not the deafening explosions of bombs, but the gentle sound of the monsoon rain.

For Mrs. Na

American veterans have also returned to Vietnam since the end of the war: some to help in projects of reconciliation and reconstruction, including a Peace Park in My Lai; others for more personal reasons. Among them were three poets, John Balaban, Bruce Weigl, and W. D. Ehrhart. Weigl and Ehrhart and both served in the military; Balaban was a civilian aid worker. They were, Ehrhart has written, "just three poets who wanted to see with our own eyes Vietnam the country, not Vietnam the war." In this poem, For Mrs. Na, Ehrhart describes his encounter with one of the mothers whose sons he had fought against.

For Mrs. Na
Cu Chi District
December 1985

I always told myself,
if I ever got the chance to go back,
I'd never say "I'm sorry"
to anyone. Christ,
those guys I saw on television once:
sitting in Hanoi, the cameras rolling,
crying, blubbering
all over the place. Sure,
I'm sorry. I never meant
to do the things I did.
But that was nearly twenty years ago:
enough's enough.
If I ever go back
I always told myself,
I'll hold my head steady
and look them in the eye.
But here I am at last—
and here you are.
And you lost five sons in the war,
And you haven't any left.
And I'm staring at my hands
and eating tears,
trying to think of something else to say
besides "I'm sorry."

Timeline

Sept. 2, 1945
Ho Chi Minh proclaims the Democratic Republic of Vietnam

Sept. 26, 1945
First American, OSS officer A. Peter Dewey, is killed in Vietnam

Dec. 19, 1946
French–Vietnamese talks break down; first Indochina War breaks out

June 5, 1948
Bao Dai named head of state by the French

May 1, 1950
President Harry S. Truman offers U.S. aid to the French in Indochina

Dec. 30, 1950
The United States, France, Vietnam, Cambodia, and Laos sign a Mutual Defense Assistance Agreement

May 7, 1954
Vietnamese defeat the French at Dien Bien Phu

May 8, 1954
Geneva Conference convenes

July 21, 1954
Geneva Accords signed

Sept. 8, 1954
The United States establishes the Southeast Asia Treaty Organization (SEATO)

July 6, 1955
Ngo Dinh Diem renounces the Geneva Accords

Dec. 20, 1960
National Liberation Front (NLF) established

Dec. 31, 1961
Approximately 3,200 U.S. servicemen in Vietnam

Dec. 31, 1962
Approximately 11,300 U.S. servicemen in Vietnam

Nov. 2, 1963
Ngo Dinh Diem and Ngo Dinh Nhu are assassinated

Nov. 23, 1963
President John F. Kennedy is assassinated

Dec. 31, 1963
Approximately 16,300 U.S. servicemen in Vietnam

Aug. 2, 1964
U.S.S. *Maddox* attacked in the Gulf of Tonkin

Aug. 4, 1964
U.S.S. *Turner Joy* allegedly attacked in the Gulf of Tonkin

Aug. 7, 1964
U.S. Congress passes the Tonkin Gulf Resolution

Dec. 31, 1964
Approximately 23,300 U.S. servicemen in Vietnam

Mar. 2, 1965
Operation Rolling Thunder unleashed

Mar. 24, 1965
First "teach-in" against the war on a college campus (University of Michigan)

Dec. 31, 1965
Approximately 184,300 U.S. servicemen in Vietnam as well as 22,500 "allied" troops

Dec. 31, 1966
Approximately 385,200 U.S. servicemen in Vietnam

the United States

men in Vietnam

Sept. 3, 1967
Nguyen Van Thieu "elected" president of South Vietnam in a dubious electoral process

Dec. 31, 1967
Approximately 485,600 U.S. servicemen in Vietnam

Jan. 30, 1968
Tet offensive launched

Mar. 16, 1968
My Lai massacre occurs

May 12, 1968
Paris Peace Talks begin

Dec. 31, 1968
Approximately 536,000 U.S. servicemen in Vietnam

Jan. 22, 1969
Richard M. Nixon becomes President of

Sept. 3, 1969
Ho Chi Minh dies

Dec. 31, 1969
Approximately 475,200 U.S. servicemen in Vietnam

Feb. 20, 1970
Henry Kissinger begins secret peace talks with the North Vietnamese in Paris

Apr. 30, 1970
The United States invades Cambodia

Dec. 31, 1970
Approximately 334,600 U.S. servicemen in Vietnam

June 13, 1971
New York Times publishes the Pentagon Papers

Dec. 31, 1971
Approximately 156,800 U.S. service-

Oct. 11, 1972
Kissinger and his Vietnamese counterparts reach an agreement to end the war

Dec. 18–29, 1972
The United States launches massive bombing of Hanoi (the "Christmas bombing") to convince the South Vietnamese that the secretly negotiated peace treaty will not mean an end to U.S. military support

Dec. 31, 1972
Approximately 24,000 U.S. servicemen in Vietnam

Jan. 27, 1973
The United States, South Vietnam, National Liberation Front, and North Vietnam sign a peace treaty in Paris

Feb.–Mar., 1973
North Vietnam releases U.S. prisoners of war

Aug. 14, 1973
All U.S. military operations in Indochina end

Dec. 31, 1973
Approximately 50 U.S. servicemen in Vietnam

Dec. 13, 1974
Battles break out between the armies of North and South Vietnam

Apr. 12, 1975
President Nguyen Van Thieu resigns

Apr. 29–30, 1975
North Vietnamese troops take Saigon and the war ends

Glossary

ARVN—Army of the Republic of Vietnam (South). Regular army units of the south.

attrition—A policy or strategy with the goal of killing as many of the enemy as possible, rather than fighting for territory.

body count—enemy casualty statistics regularly reported by the military to the press as a measure of U.S. military success; the numerical expression of a policy of attrition.

casualty—A person either wounded or killed in action. The general category includes prisoners and those who later died of their wounds.

CIA—Central Intelligence Agency of the United States.

DMZ—Demilitarized zone along the 17th parallel dividing South Vietnam from North Vietnam.

DRV—The Democratic Republic of Vietnam; capitol in Hanoi.

frag killing—one's own officer, sometimes with a fragmentation grenade.

Free Fire Zone—Area from which friendly civilians were supposed to have been cleared; anyone found may be killed.

GVN—Government of Vietnam; capitol in Saigon (see also RVN).

KIA—Killed in action.

MACV—Military Assistance Command, Vietnam.

MIA—Missing in action.

NLF—National Liberation Front; the umbrella organization formed in the South in 1961 to fight against the Diem government and the United States. Commonly referred to as the Viet Cong (VC) by the U.S. and the South Vietnamese government.

North Vietnam—The colloquial name for the Democratic Republic of Vietnam.

PAVN—People's Army of Vietnam (North); regular army units from the north, sometimes referred to as the NVA.

Pentagon Papers—The secret history of U.S. involvement in Vietnam from 1945 to 1967; leaked to the press by Daniel Ellsberg in 1971.

POW—Prisoner of war.

punji stick—Sharpened bamboo sticks that were stuck in the ground and used as booby traps in the countryside by NLF forces.

RVN—The Republic of Vietnam; capital in Saigon.

search and destroy—The active pursuit of guerillas in the countryside, one aspect of the strategy of attrition.

South Vietnam—Colloquial name for the Republic of Vietnam.

Viet Cong (VC)—"Vietnamese Communists"; phrase used by the U.S. and the Saigon government to refer to the NLF.

vietnamization—The gradual transition of military ground control in South Vietnam from American troops to South Vietnamese troops.

Further Reading and Web Sites

Overviews of the Vietnam War

Appy, Christian G. *The Working-Class War.* Chapel Hill: University of North Carolina Press, 1993.

Emerson, Gloria. *Winners and Losers: Battles, Retreats, Gains, Losses, and Ruins from the Vietnam War.* New York: Norton, 1992.

Herr, Michael. *Dispatches.* New York: Knopf, 1977.

Herring, George. *America's Longest War, the United States and Vietnam, 1950–1975.* 3rd ed. New York: McGraw Hill, 1995.

Karnow, Stanley. *Vietnam: A History.* 2nd ed. New York: Penguin, 1997.

McNamara, Robert and Brian Vandemark. *In Retrospect: The Tragedy and Lessons of Vietnam.* New York: Times, 1995.

Sheehan, Neil. *The Bright and Shining Lie: John Paul Vann and America in Vietnam.* New York: Random House, 1988.

Young, Marilyn B. *The Vietnam Wars, 1945–1990.* New York: HarperCollins, 1991.

Origins of the Vietnam War

Anderson, David L. *Trapped By Success: The Eisenhower Administration and the Vietnam War, 1953–1961.* New York: Columbia University Press, 1991.

Gardner, Lloyd. *Approaching Vietnam: From World War II through Dienbienphu, 1941–1954.* New York: Norton, 1988.

Kennedy's War

Chomsky, Noam. *Rethinking Camelot.* Boston: South End Press, 1993.

Halberstam, David. *The Best and the Brightest.* New York: Ballantine, 1993.

Logevall, Frederik. *Choosing War: The Lost Chance for Peace and the Escalation of the War in Vietnam.* Berkeley: University of California Press, 1999.

Johnson's War

Gardner, Lloyd. *Pay Any Price: Lyndon Johnson and the Wars for Vietnam.* Chicago: Ivan R. Dee, 1995.

Kahin, George McTurnan. *Intervention: How America Became Involved in Vietnam.* New York: Knopf, 1986.

Nixon's War

Berman, Larry. *No Peace, No Honor: Nixon, Kissinger, and Betrayal in Vietnam.* New York: Free Press, 2001.

Franklin, H. Bruce. *M.I.A. or Mythmaking in America.* New Brunswick, N.J.: Rutgers University Press, 1993.

The Antiwar Movement and the Sixties

Anderson, Terry. *The Sixties.* New York: Longman, 1999.

Hunt, Andrew. *The Turning: A History of Vietnam Veterans Against the War.* New York: NYU Press, 2001.

Wells, Tom. *The War Within: America's Battle over Vietnam.* Berkeley: University of California Press, 1994.

Biography

Bradley, Benjamin. *Conversations with Kennedy.* New York: Norton, 1975.

Dallek, Robert. *Flawed Giant: Lyndon B. Johnson, 1960–1973.* New York: Oxford University Press, 1998.

Duiker, William J. *Ho Chi Minh.* New York: Hyperion, 2000.

Reeves, Richard. *President Nixon: Alone in the White House.* News York: Simon & Schuster, 2001.

Poetry, Memoirs, Fiction

Bao Ninh. *The Sorrow of War: A Novel of North Vietnam.* Translated from the Vietnamese by Phan Thanh Hao. New York: Riverhead, 1996.

Bowen, Kevin and Bruce Weigl, eds. *Writing Between the Lines: An Anthology on War and its Social Consequences.* Amherst: University of Massachusetts Press, 1997.

Carroll, James. *An American Requiem: God, My Father, and the War That Came.* Boston: Houghton Mifflin, 1997.

Ehrhart, W. D. *Carrying Darkness: The Poetry of the Vietnam War.* Lubbock: Texas Tech University Press, 1989.

Franklin, H. Bruce, ed. *The Vietnam War in American Stories, Songs and Poems*. New York: Bedford, 1996.

Hayslip, Le Ly, and Jay Wurts. *When Heaven and Earth Changed Places: A Vietnamese Woman's Journey from War to Peace*. New York: Plume, 1993.

Mariscal, George, ed. *Aztlan and Viet Nam: Chicano and Chicana Experiences of the Vietnam War*. Berkeley: University of California Press, 1999.

Palmer, Laura. *Shrapnel in the Heart: Letters and Remembrances from the Vietnam Veterans Memorial*. New York: Vintage, 1988.

Truong, Nhu Tang, with David Chanoff and Doan Van Toai. *A Viet Cong Memoir: An Inside Account of the Vietnam War and its Aftermath*. New York: Vintage, 1986.

Women at War

Turner, Karen G. and Phan Thanh Hao. *Even the Women Must Fight: Memories of War from North Vietnam*. New York: John Wiley, 1999.

Van Devanter, Lynda, with Charles Morgan. *Home Before Morning: the Story of an Army Nurse in Vietnam*. New York: Warner, 1984.

African Americans at War

Terry, Wallace, ed. *Bloods: an Oral History of the Vietnam War by Black Veterans*. New York: Random House, 1984.

Westheider, James E. *Fighting on Two Fronts: African Americans and the Vietnam War*. New York: NYU Press, 1997.

Documentary Collections

Cohen, Steven, ed. *Anthology and Guide to a Television History*. New York: Knopf, 1983.

Katsiaficas, George, ed. *Vietnam Documents: American and Vietnamese Views of the War*. Armonk, New York: M.E. Sharpe, 1992.

Olson, James S. and Randy Roberts. *My Lai: a Brief History with Documents*. Boston: Bedford, 1998.

Pratt, John Clark, compiler. *Vietnam Voices: Perspectives on the War Years, 1941–1975*. Athens: University of Georgia Press, 1999.

Web Sites

A Different War
http://www.nytimes.com/library/world/asia/vietnam-war-index.html

Articles, maps, and resources from the *New York Times* database.

Documents Relating to American Foreign Policy
http://www.mtholyoke.edu/acad/intrel/vietnam.htm

Comprehensive database of documents concerning the Vietnam War.

House Committee on Veterans' Affairs
http://ww.house.gov/va/vets/war/vietnam.htm

The House Committee on Veterans' Affairs site on the Vietnam war.

Presidential Libraries
http://www.nara.gov/nara/president/address.html

Listing of U.S. Presidential libraries that are part of the National Archives and Records.

Recalling the Vietnam War
http://globetrotter.berkeley.edu/PubEd/research/vietnam.html

Major voices from the Vietnam era discuss U.S. foreign policy during the war.

"Vietnam: A Television History"
http://www.pbs.org/wgbh/amex/vietnam/

Companion website to the *The American Experience* series on the Vietnam War.

Vietnam Declassification Project
http://www.ford.utexas.edu/library/exhibits/vietnam/vietnam.htm

Documents from the Vietnam Declassification Project at the Ford Library.

Vietnam Veterans of America
http://www.vva.org/
Vietnam Veterans of America home page.

Vietnam Veterans Memorial
http://www.nps.gov/vive/index.htm
Official Vietnam Veterans Memorial site.

Text Credits

Front Matter and Introduction

9: Copyright ©1969, Tom Lehrer.

19: Mark Philip Bradley, trans., *Imaging Vietnam and America: The Making of Postcolonial Vietnam 1919–1950* (Chapel Hill: University of North Carolina Press, 2000), 18.

20–21: Department of State, National Archives, Washington, D.C., 851G.00/1.

22–23: Tran Van Don, *Our Endless War: Inside Vietnam* (San Rafael, California, London: Presidio, 1978), 8–10.

Chapter 1

27–29: Ho Chi Minh, *Selected Works*, vol. 3 (Hanoi: Foreign Languages Publishing House, 1960, 1962), 17–21.

30: Charles Fenn, *Ho Chi Minh: A Biographical Introduction* (New York: Scribners, 1973), 83.

30–31: Department of State, National Archives, Washington, D.C., 851G.oo/2-2046.

32–34: *United States–Vietnam Relations, 1945–1967: Study Prepared by Department of Defense*, book 8, printed for the use of the House Committee on Armed Services (Washington, D.C.: Government Printing Office, 1971), 144–148.

34–36: George Kennan, *Memoirs, 1950–1963* (New York: Little Brown, 1972), 58–60. Copyright © 1972, George F. Kennan.

36–37: Telegram from Dean Acheson to the U.S. Consulate in Hanoi, May 20, 1949, in *Foreign Relations of the United States, 1949*, vol. 7 (Washington, D.C.: Government Printing Office, 1975), 29–30.

37–38: "The President's News Conference of April 7, 1954, Number 73," in *Public Papers of the Presidents of the United States: Dwight D. Eisenhower, 1954* (Washington, D.C.: Government Printing Office, 1960), 382–383.

38–39: Luther A. Huston, "High Aide Says Troops Must Be Sent if the French Withdraw," *New York Times*, April 17, 1954, 1, 3.

Chapter 2

42: Words and music by Pete Seeger. TRO Copyright © 1967 (renewed) Melody Trails, Inc. Used by permission.

44–46: *Department of State Bulletin*, 31:788, August 2, 1954, 164.

46: *Department of State Bulletin*, 31:788, August 2, 1954, 162–163.

46–47: "Statement Regarding the Agreements of the Geneva Conference by Premier Ngo Dinh Diem,

July 22, 1954." In *The Reunification of Vietnam* (Saigon: Ministry of Information, 1958), 29.

47–48: Ho Chi Minh, "Long Live Peace, Unity, Independence, and Democracy in Vietnam, July 30, 1954." In *For a Lasting Peace, For a People's Democracy* (Bucharest: Communist Information Bureau, 1954), 3.

49–50: *Department of State Bulletin*, 31:803, November 15, 1954, 735–736.

51–53: Edward G. Lansdale to Maxwell D. Taylor, "Lansdale Team's Report on Covert Saigon Mission in 1954 and 1955." In *The Senator Gravel Edition. The Pentagon Papers: The Defense Department History of United States Decision-making on Vietnam*, vol. 2 (Boston: Beacon, 1971–1972), 643–649.

53–56: Truong Nhu Tang, with David Chanoff and Doan Van Toai, *A Viet Cong Memoir: An Inside Account of the Vietnam War and Its Aftermath* (New York: Vintage, 1986), 37–40. Copyright © 1985 Truong Nhu Tang, David Chanoff, and Doan Van Toai. Reprinted by permission of Georges Borchardt, Inc., on behalf of the authors.

57–58: Liberation Radio/South Vietnam, February 13–14, 1961. In *Foreign Broadcast Information Service. Far East. Daily Reports* (North Vietnam), No. 30, February 14, 1961, EEE3–EEE10.

59–60: *Inaugural Addresses of the Presidents of the United States* (Washington, D.C.: Government Printing Office, 1989), 306.

61–63: *Reporting Vietnam: Part One: American Journalism 1959–1969* (New York: Library of America, 1998), 79–83. Copyright © 1965, 1968, Malcom Browne.

64–65: *The Senator Gravel Edition. The Pentagon Papers. The Defense Department's History of U.S. Decision-making on Vietnam*, vol. 2 (Boston: Beacon, 1971–1972), 735, 789–792, 793.

Chapter 3

67–69: *Foreign Relations of the United States, 1961–1963. Vietnam, August–December 1963* (Washington, D.C.: Government Printing Office, 1991), 732–734.

70: David M. Barrett, ed. *Lyndon B. Johnson's Vietnam Papers: A Documentary Collection* (College Station: Texas A&M University Press, 1997), 21.

71–72: Michael R. Beschloss, ed., *Taking Charge: The Johnson White House Tapes, 1963–1964* (New York: Simon & Schuster, 1997), 401–403. Copyright © 1997 by Michael R. Beschloss.

73–75: *Department of State Bulletin*, 51:1313, August 24, 1964, 259.

75–77: Jim and Sybil Stockdale, *In Love and War*, revised and updated (Annapolis: Naval Institute Press, 1990), 19–25.

77–78: William Appleman Williams, Thomas McCormick, Lloyd Gardner, and Walter LaFeber, ecrt., *America in Vietnam* (New York: Norton, 1985), 236–239. vol. 2 (Washington, D.C.: Government Printing Office, 1996), 427.

78: Department of State Bulletin No. 51:1313, August 24, 1964 1268.

79–80: *Foreign Relations of the U.S., Vietnam, January–June 1965*, vol. 2 (Washington, D.C.: Government Printing Office, 1996), 181–185.

81–82: *The Senator Gravel Edition. The Pentagon Papers: The Defense Department History of United States Decision-making on Vietnam*, vol 4 (Boston: Beacon, 1971), 606–624.

82–84: *The Senator Gravel Edition. The Pentagon Papers: The Defense Department History of United States Decision-making on Vietnam*, vol. 4 (Boston: Beacon, 1971), 606–624.

84–85: Lyndon B. Johnson, "The President's News Conference of July 28, 1965," No. 388, in *Public Papers of the Presidents of the United States: Lyndon B. Johnson, 1965, Book 1* (Washington, D.C.: Government Printing Office, 1966), 794–795.

86–87: *Who, What, When, Where, Why: Report from Vietnam by Walter Cronkite*, broadcast February 27, 1968. Copyright © 1968, CBS Inc.

Chapter 5

98–99: SSS Form 252 (Revised 4-28-65), Selective Service System, Washington, D.C.

99–100: Larry Rottman, *Voices from the Ho Chi Minh Trail* (Desert Hot Springs, Calif.: Event Horizon Press, 1993), 11.

100–101: *Poems from Captured Documents*. Selected and translated by Thanh T. Nguyen and Bruce Weigl (Amherst: University of Massachusetts Press, 1994), 45–47.

101–103: Truong Nhu Tang, with David Chanoff and Doan Van Toai, *A Viet Cong Memoir: An Inside Account of the Vietnam War and Its Aftermath* (New York: Vintage, 1986), 157–171. Copyright © 1985 Truong Nhu Tang, David Chanoff, and Doan Van Toai. Reprinted by permission of Georges Borchardt, Inc., on behalf of the authors.

103–105: Tim O'Brien, *The Things They Carried. A Work of Fiction* (New York: Penguin, 1990), 6–9. Copyright © 1980, Tim O'Brien.

106–109: Courtesy of John J. Fitzgerald.

109: Michael Casey, *Obscenities* (New York: Warner, 1972), 43. Copyright © 1972, Michael Casey.

110: Katsuichi Honda, *Vietnam—A Voice From The Villages* (Senjo no Mura) (Tokyo, Japan: Committee for the English Publication of Vietnam—A Voice

From the Villages, 1968), 14–15.

110–111: Keith Walker, *A Piece of My Heart: The Stories of Twenty-six American Women Who Served in Vietnam* (New York: Ballantine, 1985), 45–46.

113: *The Dellums Committee Hearings on War Crimes in Vietnam: An Inquiry into Command Responsibility in Southeast Asia*. Ed. Citizens Commission of Inquiry (New York: Vintage, 1972), 283.

114–115: B. Drummond Ayers, "Army is Shaken by Crisis in Morale and Discipline," *New York Times*, September 5, 1971, 1, 36.

Chapter 6

118–119: Quoted in Thomas Hauser, *Muhhamad Ali: His Life and Times* (New York: Simon & Schuster, 1991), 171–172. Copyright © 1991, Thomas Hauser and Muhhamad Ali.

119–122: James Melvin Washington, ed., *I Have a Dream—Writings and Speeches that Changed the World* (New York, NY: HarperCollins, 1992), 135–152. Copyright © 1963, Martin Luther King; renewed © 1991, Coretta Scott King. Reprinted with arrangement with the Estate of Martin Luther King Jr., c/o Writer's House.

123–124: George Breitman, ed. *Malcolm X Speaks* (New York: Grove, 1965), 218–219. Copyright © 1965, 1989, Betty Shabazz and Pathfinder Press.

124–127: John Kerry Speech, April 22, 1971. In *Congressional Record*, May 3, 1971.

Chapter 7

132: *The Peers Inquiry of the Massacre at My Lai*, vol. 2, book 8 (Bethesda, Maryland: Vietnam War Research Collections, Congressional Information Service, 1999), 10–12.

132–133: *The Peers Inquiry of the Massacre at My Lai*. vol. 2, book 24 (Bethesda, MD: Vietnam War Research Collections, Congressional Information Service, 1999), 31–33.

133–135: Seymour Hersh, "Lieutenant Accused of Murdering 109 Civilians," *St. Louis Post-Dispatch*, November 13, 1969, 1, 19.

135: Seymour Hersh, "Hamlet Attack Called 'Point-Blank Murder,'" *St. Louis Post-Dispatch*, November 20, 1969, 1, 16. Copyright © 1969.

135: Seymour Hersh, "Ex-GI Tells of Killing Civilians at Pinkville," *St. Louis Post-Dispatch*, November 25, 1969, 1, 9.

135–136: "The Great Atrocity Hunt," *National Review*, December 16, 1969, 1252. Copyright © 1969, *National Review*.

136–138: Richard Nixon, *RN: The Memoirs of Richard Nixon* (New York: Simon & Schuster, 1978), 409.

138–139: *Public Papers of the Presidents of the United States: Richard Nixon, Containing the public messages, speeches, and statements of the President* (Washington,

D.C.: Government Printing Office, 1971–1975), 405–409.

139–141: *The Report of the President's Commission on Campus Unrest.* (Washington, DC: Government Printing Office, 1970), pp. 17–20, 47–48, 272–274, 429–430, 459.

141–143: Gaylord Nelson, "The Tragedy of Vietnam," *Milwaukee Journal*, February 25, 1972, 15.

145: Gareth Porter, *Vietnam: A History in Documents* (New York: New American Library, 1981), 424.

Chapter 8

149–151. Bill McCloud, ed., *What Should We Tell Our Children About Vietnam?* (Norman: University of Oklahoma Press, 1989), 56–59. Copyright © 1989, Larry Heinemann. Reprinted by permission of Ellen Levine Literary Agency, Inc.

151–152: Robert S. McNamara, *In Retrospect: The Tragedy and Lessons of Vietnam* (New York: Times Books, 1995), xv–xvi.

152–153: B. Drummond Ayers, "Belated Regrets About Vietnam Create A Consensus of Antipathy," *New York Times*, April 15, 1995, 7.

153–154: Dean Rusk, as told to Richard Rusk, *As I Saw It* (New York: Norton, 1990), 492–493, 497, 502. Reprinted with the permission of Russel & Volkening. Copyright ©1990, Dean Rusk.

155–157: Bruce Weigl, "Welcome Home," *The Nation*, November 27, 1982, 549.

157–159: Robert S. McNamara, James G. Blight, and Robert K. Brigham, *Argument Without End: In Search of Answers to the Vietnam Tragedy* (New York: Public Affairs, 1999), 81–82, 84–87, 94.

160–161: Elliot, Duong Van Mai, *The Sacred Willow* (New York: Oxford University Press, 1999), 496–474.

Sidebar Text

31: Isaacs, Harold Robert, *New Cycle in Asia* (New York: Macmillian, 1947).

60: Words and music by S. Sgt. Barry Sadler and Robin Moore/Eastaboga Music.

75: Interview of Secretary of State Dean Rusk by Elie Abel of NBC television, broadcast on August 5, 1964. In *Department of State Bulletin* 51:1313, August 24, 1964, 269.

76: Michael Beschloss, ed., *Taking Charge. The Johnson White House Tapes, 1963–1964* (New York: Simon & Schuster, 1997), 493–494.

77: Speech to National Association of Counties, Washington, D.C., August 10, 1964. In *Vital Speeches of the Day* 30:22, (September 1, 1964), 676–678.

78: Wayne Morse speech. In *Congressional Record–Senate*, February 29, 1968, 4691.

81: Assistant Secretary of Defense for International

Security Affairs, John T. McNaugton, *Foreign Relations, Vietnam, 1964–1968. January–June 1965.*

86: David Halberstam, *The Powers That Be* (New York: Knopf, 1979), 514.

110: Martha Hess, *Then the Americans Came: Voices from Vietnam* (New York: Four Walls Eight Windows, 1993), 47–48.

113: Richard Severo, "The Journalist," *Modern Maturity* 43W3:3, May–June 2000, 44–46. Copyright © 2000, AARP.

118: Copyright © 1965, Joe McDonald; renewed ©1993 by Alkatraz Corner Music/BMI.

119: Copyright © 1970 (renewed), Sony/ATV songs.

121: Donald Duncan, "The Whole Thing Was a Lie," *Ramparts* 4:10, February 1966, 13–24.

125: David H. Hackworth, "The Point Man," *Modern Maturity* 43W:3, May–June 2000, 43, 84. Copyright © 2000, AARP.

126: *Vital Speeches of the Day* 34:6, (January 1, 1968), 174–176.

131: H. R. Haldeman and Joseph DiMona, *The End of Power* (New York: Times Books, 1978), 83.

134: *Newsweek*, April 12, 1971, 28. Copyright © 1971, Newsweek, Inc.

136: Martha Hess, *Then the Americans Came: Voices from Vietnam* (New York: Four Walls Eight Windows, 1993), 129–130. Copyright ©1993, Martha Hess.

137: H. R. Haldeman, *The Haldeman Diaries: Inside the Nixon White House* (New York: Berkley Edition, 1995), 118–121; 128–130.

141: H. R. Haldeman, *The Haldeman Diaries: Inside the Nixon White House*. New York, Berkley Edition, 1995), 194–195.

143: Anthony Lewis, "Vietnam Delenda Est," *New York Times*, December 23, 1972, 25.

145: Daniel Ellsberg, "What I Had to Do," *Modern Maturity* 43W:3, May–June 2000, 84. Copyright © 2000, AARP.

149: *Public Papers of the Presidents of the United States: Ronald Reagan, 1988–1989*, vol. II (Washington, DC: United States Government Printing Office, 1991), 1495–1496.

153: David Halberstam, "Vietnam: Why We Missed the Story," *Washington Post National Weekly Edition*, May 22–28, 1995, 8–9.

157: Copyright © 1984, Bruce Springsteen (ASCAP). Reprinted by permission.

161: W. D. Ehrhart, *Beautiful Wreckage: New and Selected Poems* (East Hampton, Mass.: Adastra Press 1999), 110.

Picture Credits

Agence France-Press: 19; AP/WIDE WORLD PHOTO: 43, 112; Courtesy of Authors: 58, 85, 86, 99, 103, 108, 111, 124, 142; Marty Baldessari: 156; © Bettman/CORBIS: 9; *Boston Globe*: 72; Branger-Voillet: 15, 162; confucious.org: 12; Cornell University Library, The Making of America Digital Collection; (Original Source: The Century, Vol. 32, Issue 3, page 416): 10; *Daily News of Los Angeles*: 9; © John A. Darnell, Jr.: 143; Department of Defense: 84, 163; *Fayetteville Observer*: 60; John J. Fitzgerald: contents page, 107, 163; Foreign Language Press: 91 *top*; Courtesy of A. Tom Grunfeld: 47, 48, 79, 159; Courtesy of Dirck Halstead: 146; Jane Yett Kiely: 143; Ngo Vinn Long Collection: 29, 95 *bottom*; *Los Angeles Times*: 134; Library of Congress (LC-USZ62-109514) 14, (NYWTS, 1/4/67, VIETNAM...HISTORY) 23, (LC-USZ62-108454) 27, (LC-USZ62-126868 34, (acd 2a10370) 37, (NYWTS, 8/3/64, U.S...NAVY.. VESSELS..MADDOX) 74, (LC-USZ62-90350) 77, (LC-YSZC4-3860) 88, (POS 6-U.S., no. 391 [C Size]) 89, (POS 6-U.S., no. 1455 [C size]) 93, (POS 6-U.S., no. 681 [C size]) 114,

(LC-USZ62-129641) 118, (LC-USZ62-115431)119, (LC-USZ62-111164) 121, (POS 6-U.S., no. 279 [C size]) 123, (NYWTS, 4/4/67) 127, (LC-L917-65-2567, #2) 130, (LC-USZ62-127178) 133, (LC-USZ62-126776) 135, (POS 6-U.S., no. 195 [C size]) 137, 140, (POS 6-U.S., no. 804 [C size]) 144, (LC-USZ62-102948) 151, (LC-USZ62-109514) 162, (POS 6-U.S., no. 1455 [C size]) 163; Marvel Comics: 94; *Miami Daily News*: 148; National Archives: (NWDNS-111-C-CC47777) cover, (NWDNS-111-SC-635974) 2, (306-NT-94A-11) 24, (NWCTM-226-ENT140-HOCHIMINHLTR) 26, (W&C#383) 32, (80-G-652364) 40, (59-G-VS-3130-57) 45, (NWDNS-342-AF-18302USAF) 49, (NWDNS-342-C-KE35295) 51, (NLK-POF-SPEECHFILE-INAUGURALADD-5FFF) 59, (NLK-POF-CNTRYS-VTNMGNRAL1963-WHTELDIEMTOPRES) 64, (NLK-NSF-MM-MTGONVIETNM-DOSITLODGETOSEC) 65, (NLJ-WHPO-A-VN137) 66, (NWDNS-342-AF-107064USAF) 70, (NLJ-WHPO-A-VN049) 71, (NLJ-WHPO-A-VN013) 73, (NLJ-WHPO-A-

VN076) 80, (NWDNS-111-SC-613587) 83, (NWDNS-111-SC-646675) 87, (NWDNS-111-SC-631523) 93, (NWDNS-111-SC-647323) 96, (NWDNS-111-SC-636742) 101, (NWDNS0127-N-A186578) 104, (NWDNS-111-SC-661880) 105, (NWDNS-428-N-1115448) 110, (NWDNS-111-C-CC59950) 113, (NLJ-WHPO-A-VN123) 116, (NLNP-WHPO-MPF-1631(12)]) 128, (NLNP-WHPO-MPF-3448(21A]) 138; North Vietnam News Agency: 57; Pathfinder Press/Photo taken from Out Now!, Flax Hermes: 120; Pilgrim Press, 90 *bottom*, 92 *top, middle*; Steve Rees, 92 *bottom*; Roget-Voillet: 63; Mel Rosenthal: 160; © Edward Sorel: 61; Gary Tong: 69; U.S. Government, Military Assistance Command, Vietnam, 99, 108; © Vietnam Veterans Against the War, Inc.: 90 *bottom*; Yale University Library, Maurice Durand Collection: 16; Courtesy of Marilyn Young: 30, 90, 154, 155, 171, 172, 175, 176, 178, 185, 188, 189, 190, 192, 196, 197. Young Americans for Freedom: 93 *bottom*.

Index